YOUR NEIGHBORS DID WHAT!

A Practical, Plain English Consumer Guide

For Resolving Neighborhood Disputes

By Frederic White

© 2016

TABLE OF CONTENTS

Preface

Acknowledgements

Chapter I   **Resolving Neighborhood Disputes**

         What Makes a Good Neighbor? pg. 2

         Governing Rules for Neighbors pg. 3

         Unwritten Rules: The "Common Law" pg. 3

         Local Ordinances, including Zoning pg. 4

         State Law, including Zoning pg. 5

         Neighborhood Associations & HOAs pg.7

         Deed Covenants & Restrictions pg.9

         One-on One Discussions pg.10

         Connecting with Your Neighbors pg.11

         Letters and Social Media pg.11

         Local Officials pg.12

         The Courts pg. 13

             Filing Fees pg. 13

             Transportation, Fuel & Parking Costs pg.14

             Timing and Delays pg. 14

             Small Claims Courts pg.15

Alternate Dispute Resolution pg. 17

Lawyers pg. 18

Chapter II **Making Your Point**

Create a List   pg. 20

Find the Right Party   pg. 21

Learn the Law pg. 22

Talking to Your Other Neighbors   pg. 22

Approaching the Problem Neighbor pg. 23

Assemble the Necessary Documentation pg. 25

Promptness pg.27

Appropriate Dress pg. 27

Staying Calm pg. 28

Practice Your Argument pg. 28

Chapter III **Noise and Neighbors**

Noise Law Generally pg. 30
Anti-Noise Legislation pg. 31
State Anti-Noise Laws pg. 32

Local Anti-Noise Laws pg.32

Noise Prohibitions in Rental Agreements pg. 33

Restrictive Covenants   pg. 35

Remedies   pg. 35

Approaching Your Neighbor   pg. 35

Warning Your Neighbor   pg. 35

ADR (Mediation) pg. 37

Police Involvement   pg. 37

Litigation (Suing for Nuisance) pg. 38

Questions and Answers   pg. 39

Chapter IV   Dog Law

Dog Law Generally pg. 45

Local Dog Laws   pg. 45

At-Large Dogs & Impoundment   pg. 46

Dog Leashing and Control   pg. 47

Licenses   pg. 48

Disease Control   pg.48

Control of Animal Waste   pg.48

Dangerous Dog Ordinances   pg.487

Questions and Answers   pg. 49

Chapter V **Fences**

Fence Law Basics   pg. 58

Construction and Maintenance pg. 59

Partition or Division Fences   pg. 60

Partition Fence Agreements pg. 60

Fence Removal or Destruction pg. 60

Statutory Fence Law   pg. 61

Questions and Answers pg. 62

Chapter VI   Adjoining Landowners

Adjoining Landowners Generally pg. 71

Boundaries   pg. 71

Permissible Uses of Property pg. 73

Trees, Branches, and Roots pg. 74

Other Encroachments pg. 75

Lateral and Subjacent Support pg. 75

Prohibitions Against Storage of Dangerous Substances   pg. 76

Easements for Light, Air & View pg. 76

Avoiding Dangers to Your Neighbors pg. 78

Questions and Answers pg. 79

Chapter VII   Trespassers

Trespass Law Generally pg. 88

Types of Civil Trespassers pg. 89

    People Who Take "Shortcuts" pg. 89

    People Who Use Your Property's Amenities pg. 89

    People Who Encroach Upon Your Property   pg. 90

Children and Trespassing pg. 90

Prerequisites to a Successful Trespass Action   pg. 92

Actions for Damages for Trespass   pg. 93

Types of Damages Awards Available pg. 94

Mistaken Trespass pg. 97

Persons Liable for Trespass pg. 98

Defenses to a Trespass Action pg. 98

Questions and Answers pg. 98

Chapter VIII   Businesses in Residential Neighborhoods

Businesses in Your Neighborhood pg. 105

Restrictions on the Use of the Business Owner's Home   pg. 106

Restrictions on Types of Business Activities pg. 106

Nuisances and Negligence   pg. 109

Questions and Answers pg. 110

Glossary of Selected Legal Terms

Additional Resources

Appendices

About the Author

Other Books by Frederic White

PREFACE

The late Poet Laureate Carl Sandburg once wrote that "Good fences make good neighbors." Fair enough, but what happens when your neighbor's fence falls onto your property, and your neighbor won't repair it? Or suppose the fallen fence has damaged your property, including your house, and your neighbor won't pay for the damage. What then?

Or imagine if the issues affecting your property do not involve fences, but something else? What if you have loud, rowdy neighbors? Or neighbors with unruly guests, or unkempt yards? Suppose your neighbors permit unruly children and their friends to run amok? Or a neighbor's tree falls on your house? Or your neighbor's dog decides to routinely run free on your lawn and bites you, or your spouse, or one of your children? What then?

I have been answering questions like this for almost forty years since I first wrote about and practiced law in the field of property. Finally, after dealing with these inquires—usually coming from homeowners with little or no legal experience—I decided to create this basic consumer guide. It is written in plain English, and I have designed it to provide you, the average homeowner or renter, with an approach to solving real life problems with your neighbors without necessarily having you resort to the time and expense of getting sometimes-expensive legal advice.

Now don't misunderstand me. I am a trained lawyer and I highly respect the hard work lawyers do. I also understand appreciate that many of you seem to think that the only way you can solve problems with your neighbors is hire a lawyer and then resort to the courts to help you. Oftentimes, however, the solutions to the issues and problems I will be discussing can be approached in other ways, including having reasonable conversations with your neighbors, or speaking with local officials, or the officers of your local homeowners' association board, or resorting to other forms of dispute resolution before you choose to move on to the courts.

The purpose of this consumer guide is to help the average homeowner answer property dispute questions and provide some practical solutions to common problems that continue to plague many of us. Some of my suggested solutions will only require some measured, friendly conversations with your neighbors, most of whom do not really start their day just to annoy you. Often, their actions are just misguided, or simply result from some basic misunderstanding of the rules.

A few of my suggestions, however, are bound to be more complex, sometimes involving local authorities, including the police; sometimes involving the courts, or other means such as "Alternative Dispute Resolution" (ADR).

I admit that talking to your neighbors occasionally can be tough going. Gone are the days when many of us across the country grew up in urban and rural neighborhoods with houses that had front porches, where we knew our neighbors and their friends, and people talked with each other.

Today, in this age of instant electronic interaction, we rarely even know the names of our next-door neighbors, and we "communicate" through social media platforms like Facebook, Twitter, Instagram, et al. Platforms like these are hardly fit for making rational choices or engaging in reasonable problem solving.

Solving a neighborhood dispute starts by you and me **Recognizing** problem, including the limits of your neighbor's responsibility for whatever that problem is. After that, we need to **Navigate** the various roadblocks to solving the problem. Lastly, assuming we are successful in recognizing the problem and navigating our way through the steps we need to deal with it, we can **Resolve** the problem, hopefully to the mutual satisfaction of all the parties involved. I call this method of problem solving **"RNR."**

My ultimate objective in this guidebook is to provide you, the average consumer—**using a large and readable font**—with clear and concise practical answers to neighborhood dispute issues without burdening you with oft-complex references to existing state and local statutes, regulations, resolutions, and ordinances.

Other than the **Introduction** and **Making Your Point** chapters, the chapters in this consumer guide will take two basic approaches: (1) an **Explaining the Law** format—for those of you who prefer the "meat and potatoes" about the laws that affect your property in a straightforward, linear format; and (2) a **Questions and Answers** format—for those of you who feel more comfortable with getting your information by learning from real-life situations.

After reviewing these materials, you should be able to get the information you need, or at least have a roadmap for where you need to go to find additional information.

As I have indicated, the **Explaining the Law** sections of each chapter will consist of short, plain English introductory material describing the rules for each subject and providing basic information about the subject matter. What will follow in each chapter is a **Questions & Answers** section describing real-life neighborhood dispute issues and providing you with suggested answers, as well as suggestions for further action.

For those of you who want additional information, I have also included:

- A **Glossary of Selected Legal Terms**
- **Additional Resources** you might find useful, including websites and other publications.
- **Appendices** featuring checklists, forms and interesting articles about neighborhood disputes and ways to try to resolve them.

Last, but not least, I do understand that I don't have all the answers to all the questions; perhaps I may have left some out some information, or I haven't clarified something to your liking.

Fair enough! After you have reviewed this guidebook and you any have questions, comments, or suggestions, please contact me at my website: http://www.GoodNeighborsRule.com.

Now, let's get started!

Acknowledgments

Thanks to my wife, Phyllis White, for editing and providing input the tone of this consumer guide. Additional thanks to Dr. Kay Benjamin, Janna Franza Canard, and Elizabeth Hathaway, for proofing and offering editorial advice, including input on the title. Also, I thank the following people for their reviews and comments: Judge Nathaniel C. Nichols and Attorney Garrett Johnson

Chapter I
Introduction

What Makes a Good Neighbor? pg. 2
Governing Rule Basics for Neighbors pg. 3
Unwritten Rules: The "Common Law" pg. 3
Local Ordinances, including Zoning pg. 4
State Law, including Zoning pg. 5
Neighborhood Associations, including HOAs pg. 7
Deed Covenants and Restrictions pg. 9
One-on One Discussions pg. 10
Connecting with Your Neighbors pg. 11
Letters and Social Media pg. 11
Local Officials pg. 12
The Courts pg. 13
    Filing Fees pg. 13
    Transportation, Fuel & Parking Costs pg. 14
    Timing and Delays pg. 14
    Small Claims Courts p. 15
Alternate Dispute Resolution pg. 17
Lawyers pg. 18

What Makes a Good Neighbor?

What makes a good neighbor? Responses vary, but generally people across the country I speak with have told me that "good neighbors" are cordial, not abusive; helpful without being pushy; mind their own business unless requested to do otherwise; don't host parties at late hours; clean up their yards; don't let their families, including their children, run loose; nor do they let their dogs bark too long, or too loudly.

In contrast, a "bad neighbor" generally engages in activities that are the opposite of what a good neighbor does. There is a long list of "bad neighbor" activities, including:

- Excessive noise
- Disputes over boundaries, including fences and trees
- Damages caused by falling trees or encroaching tree roots
- Unruly animals, particularly dogs
- Blocked views
- Trespassing
- Unruly guests and children
- Inappropriate business activities in residential neighborhoods

All these items (and more) can produce lasting tensions, bad feelings, unnecessary confrontations, expenditures of money, litigation and—sometimes—violence.

How do we try to stop all of this?

There are many ways to resolve ordinary neighborhood disputes. They can range from having one-on-one discussions with your neighbors, working with neighborhood associations and Home Owners Associations ("HOAs"), eliciting the help of local officials, or resorting to the police and the courts. But before you take on your neighbor, you need to learn the proper guidelines for resolving disputes. So, let's start with the rules.

Governing Rule Basics for Neighbors

Unwritten Rules: The "Common Law"

Most of our American legal structure has evolved from the "Common Law," a system of judge-made law first developed in medieval England. Common Law concepts were generally based on decisions made by judges dealing with individual cases without the benefit of written rules to assist them. The development of the rules of Common Law are usually hammered into the heads of every first-year law student.

Except for Louisiana, which operates under both a Civil Law and a Common Law legal system, all United States courts derive their central rules from the Common Law. One example of the use of these rules is Common Law nuisance law. Nuisance law evolved out of the deficiencies of trespass law, and essentially stands for the idea that you should not unduly burden your neighbors by producing activities on your own property like loud noises, noxious fumes, an unkempt yard, etc.

Excellent explanations of how the Common Law developed and how it works can be found in several publications. The leading text is <u>The Common Law</u>, authored by the late United States Supreme Court Justice, Oliver Wendell Holmes. This book might be a bit lengthy for some readers. In its place, I suggest taking a look at a good, succinct explanation of the Common Law on a website like www.investopedia.cmon/terms/c/common-law.asp.

Local Ordinances, including Zoning

Most municipalities govern themselves through a combination of state laws, referred to as "statutes", and a set of local laws, usually referred to as "ordinances."

One example of a local law is the *Portland, Oregon Noise Ordinance.* It states that "No person shall operate a leaf blower in residential zones, or in the adjoining public right-of-way, between the hours of 7:00 p.m. to 7:00 a.m. the following morning, seven days a week." A Noise Control Officer administers the Portland Noise Control Ordinance. Penalties of up to $5000 can be assessed for each separate violation of the ordinance. It is highly likely that your community has a similar ordinance with respect to noise control and as well as other ordinances dealing with property owner disputes.

Today, most local government ordinances and rules can be located on your city's website. If not, your city or town clerk's office can direct you to hard copies located in your city or town hall.

Some such examples of online city code website locations are:

Carlsbad, California
www.carlsbadca.gov/cityhall/laws/codes.asp
Arlington, Texas
www.arlington-tx.gov/citysecretary/code-ordinances/
Sarasota, Florida
www.municode.com/library/Fl/Sarasota_County
Montpelier, Vermont
www.montpelier-vt.org/578/Code-of-Ordinances

A web search using your city's name and search terms like "ordinances" or "codes" should lead you to the local legislation you are seeking.

State Law, Including Zoning

Some state land-use laws often overlap, or take the place of local ordinances, including local zoning legislation, especially when it comes to matters of statewide concern such as air pollution control. Zoning is a type of land use control, first introduced in the United States in the early 1920s.

Zoning laws and your compliance with them are facts of modern life. These laws essentially have been developed to regulate land uses under the so-called governmental "Police Power." As a private citizen, you do not have the right or the power to enforce your local areas zoning laws; enforcement power is often placed in the hands of a person often referred as a "Code Enforcement Officer."

Local zoning laws control various aspects of modern living, including what property can be used for, lot sizes, types of dwellings or buildings. etc. Local zoning ordinances are often used in tandem with statewide legislation.

Similar to web searches for local ordinances, you can usually find your own state's zoning legislation by doing an online search and adding terms such as "legislation" or "statutes", etc.

Some examples of sources of state zoning legislation can be found at the following links:

Ohio
www.legislaure.ohio.gov/legislation/search-legislation
www.codes.ohio.gov.
Illinois
www.ilga.gov/legislation/ilcs/ilcs.asp
Oregon
www.oregonlegisture.gov/bills_laws/Pages/ORS.aspx
Montana
www.leg.mt.gov/bills/mca_toc/

Recognizing that it would be extremely difficult to try to oversee and regulate what goes on *inside* someone's home, zoning laws tend to concentrate on exterior factors, such as:

Excessive residential storage

Excessive vegetation and/or weeds

Junk motor vehicles

Illegal dumping

Trash, debris

Dilapidated buildings and/or structures

General building maintenance

Dilapidated fence or accessory buildings

Peeling exterior paint

Vacant, unsecured, boarded structures

Unsecured pools and spas

Neighborhood Associations, Including HOAs

Many property owners live in subdivisions, planned communities, or condominiums that are regulated by Homeowners Associations (HOAs). HOAs make and enforce rules for the properties within their jurisdictions. The rules and regulations are usually referred as "CC&Rs." If you live in one of these communities, oftentimes you can begin to seek answers to potential problems with your neighbors by reviewing the CC&Rs that affect your community. State-by-state links to HOA laws can be found at **Appendix A.**

CC&Rs cover a number of issues, including:

- Resident behavior (no glass containers around the pool; no loud parties after a certain time)
- Architecture (no fences over a certain height; no exterior house colors beyond a certain "approved" paint palette)
- Common responsibilities (fee schedules; fines for non-compliance, etc.)

CC&Rs can very restrictive, and it is important to know all the rules, as failure to do so can cost you time and money. For example, for a humorous take on some "tricky" CC&Rs, see **Appendix B.**

In addition to HOAs, some older communities still retain block clubs or similar types of neighborhood associations. In these cases, you might want to check to find out whether there are any association by-laws that you might use to solve the problem. For example, in some communities block clubs have helped set up rules about fence heights, or even house color.

Failure to abide by these kinds of rules could subject you to fines or other actions, such has having to reduce the height of your fence or take it down. If you have purchased a home and you are a member of an HOA, you should have been provided a copy of all HOA rules at closing, or prior to it. If you don't have a copy of the rules, or can't locate them, you should consult with the officers or staff of your local HOA board.

Deed Covenants and Restrictions
(Private Zoning)

Frankly, most people, even most lawyers, do not carefully review their closing documents before, during, or after closing. During even routine real property closings, there is such a flurry of initialing and signing that most people don't take the time to read materials thoroughly, often vowing to review their documents later.

Full disclosure: I have occasionally been one of those people! But it's not too late. If you are anticipating some upcoming problems with your neighbor where you suspect the violation of some deed covenants may be involved, take the time to locate your closing paperwork, including any deeds, or CC&Rs rules, or both, and review the documents. If you find that the material is too complex, you could always consult your attorney, or, in the case of CC&Rs, you could seek help from your local HOA officials.

Deed covenants and restrictions can be characterized as a kind of "private zoning." They vary greatly with respect to the issues they cover, what lands are subject to them, the length of time they will "run with the land," as well as the penalties for their violation.

"Running with the land" is a legal term that means once a land use restriction has been put in writing and filed in a public record, all "successors in interest" (subsequent purchasers) have "notice" of the restriction. That is why, typically, when you purchase a home subject to deed restrictions, you receive a hard copy of the restrictions. Receipt of these documents constitutes "notice"

Some deed covenants provide that land can never be sold for development, or that a live tree can never be cut, or a second driveway can never be constructed, or the property can never be used as a bar, or any of a huge variety of other prohibitions or requirements.

Once you know the governing rules, you will be better equipped to tackle your property problem. There are a number of approaches, some of which overlap in appropriate cases. For examples of some typical deed covenant and restrictions, see **Appendix C.**

One-on-One Discussions

The dynamic here can be tricky to navigate and personalities often come into play. If you don't have the best relationship with your neighbor to start with, and the nature of the issue you are concerned with could be touchy, then perhaps trying to have a personal conversation is not the way to go. There have been cases where long-time neighbors and friends have stopped talking to each other for extended periods of time, even forever.

Stories about feuding neighbors have become the stuff of legend. If you don't believe that you and your neighbor can have a civil, one-on-one discussion about an issue, then you should think of using other means or third parties in order to communicate.

Connecting with Your Neighbors

Remember, you are not always out there alone! Some neighbor issues, like a disputed boundary line, for example, may be personal because they only apply to you and your neighbor's property. There may be other matters—loud noises come to mind—that affect you and many others in the neighborhood. In cases like this, you might want to think about having some informal conversations with your other neighbors about the issue before you approach the offending neighbor.

If you can find common ground, you and your other neighbors' collective concern could become a powerful tool for getting the problem neighbor to discontinue the offending conduct.

Letters and Social Media

Perhaps you don't feel comfortable speaking directly with your neighbor, or your neighbor is unavailable. If so, you might prefer a more formal means like a letter, or an email. Formal letter writing, however, almost has become a lost art, and email chatter can be seriously flawed. [I am assuming here that feuding neighbors don't use social media like Instagram, Twitter, or Facebook, etc. to communicate with each other].

I often say that the email **"SEND"** button ought to stand for "**S**uspect **E**very **N**egative **D**eclaration." In short, if you think a letter or an email will get the ball rolling, it probably would be best to get an objective person to read your message **before** you send it.

Remember, once you press the "Send" button, you can't retrieve it.

Here is an example of a *possible* first letter to your neighbor:

Dear *[Neighbor]:*

As you know, a few days ago, we all felt the effects of the latest summer storm. Unfortunately, because of the storm, one of your large oak trees fell onto my home, causing damage to my roof. As I am sure you know, as the owner of the tree, you are responsible for any damages the tree causes to my property.

I am in the process of securing estimates for repairing the damage. Once I get an appropriate estimate, I would like meet with you so that we can make arrangements for the necessary repairs. I can be reached at home, or by phone at XXX-XXX-XXXX. I look forward to hearing from you.

Thank you for your cooperation.

Sincerely

[Your signature]

Local Officials

Local officials, such as city council members, can be useful in helping to resolve neighborhood disputes, especially when these disputes involve the operation of a commercial business in a primarily residential neighborhood.

For example, the business could be a convenience store that does not dispose of its garbage properly, leading to rodent and other vermin invasions. Rather than confronting the offending neighbor directly, the homeowner might be better served by directing her complaint through the council member who could serve as a buffer and who could also possess the added influence—and threat—of official action such as fines or, in extreme cases, shutting down the business.

Quite frankly, when it comes to some local officials, depending on the circumstances, the success of your dealings with them may hinge to some extent on whether you have supported them politically in the past.

The Courts

When you are trying to resolve a neighborhood dispute, you should think of courts as your last resort. Why? The answers are not necessarily obvious.

Filing Fees

Your use of the judicial system will not be free. First, there are direct costs, such as various types of filing fees, which, contingent on the jurisdiction you live in, could be substantial. Secondly, there are indirect costs to be considered, like the time you will need to expend on preparing your case. For example, if you are employed, taking the time to go to court could take time away from your job, regardless of whether you are self-employed, or you work for someone else.

You can go to your local court's website to find out what the appropriate filing fees are. In addition, you should be able to get a hard copy list of court fees from the clerk's office. Some examples of court filing fees for civil matters are as follows:

State of Oregon Circuit Courts	$252
Cook County (Chicago) Illinois	$359
Cuyahoga County, Ohio Common Pleas	$250
Milwaukee, Wisconsin Circuit Court	$269
Marion County Court (Indianapolis) Indiana	$156

Note: Court filing fees are always subject to change.

Transportation, Fuel, and Parking Costs

Additionally, you should figure out the costs of transportation. Most of us don't have the luxury of being able able to walk directly to the local courthouse. What this means is taking public transportation or driving. Both cost money. If you drive you will pay for gas, and, most likely, parking.

Timing and Delays

In addition to the issues of possible lost wages, transportation, fuel and parking costs, there is the issue of timing. While television shows like "Law and Order" convey the impression that complex legal disputes can be resolved almost overnight, that is simply not the case. Court dockets can be crowded. Don't think that because you file a lawsuit, you will have your *immediate* day in court. Unless your situation is considered to some kind of "emergency," it could be months before your claim is heard, even if your dispute involves a so-called "small claim."

Besides possible delays to getting on the court's docket, once you appear, you will still have to wait your turn. You have absolutely no control over the time the cases called ahead of yours might take. In some situations, you might have to come back another day. Lastly, even if you do have to come back, there is no guarantee that your dispute will be resolved in one court session.

Delays occur. People who forget to bring a key piece of evidence may be granted a delay, or even multiple delays if the court decides to be lenient. Moreover, if your claim is based on the alleged violation of a lease agreement, or a deed provision, and you fail to bring the necessary documentation, the court is not going to be inclined to rule in your favor. You may have to come back. And remember, the opposite side has no incentive to help you prevail!

Small Claims Courts

Many larger U.S. jurisdictions have established Small Claims Courts or Divisions to provide a more informal, expeditious and inexpensive means for individuals to pursue claims for smaller sums of money. Monetary limits vary. For example, the currently monetary limit for small claims courts in Ohio is $3,000, exclusive of interest and costs. Monetary limits are subject to change.

The majority of litigants appearing in small claims courts represent themselves, but lawyers are permitted. Be mindful that if you do not hire an attorney to represent you in your small claims case, you assume ALL RESPONSIBILITY for it.

In addition to adhering to the court's monetary claim limit, you will be required to pay a fee at the time you file your case. Further, it is generally required that the defendant (the person or business you are suing) either live or conduct business in the area of the court's jurisdiction.

When you finally appear, the court will generally require: (a) the complete names and addresses of all defendants; (b) some of proof of your small claim; (c) paid receipts, if any, and (d) written estimates of damages or loss that reflect the amount you are asking for in your claim. Although this kind information usually is not needed at the time of filing, you should be prepared with documentation, which will be presented to the small claims court judge at the hearing.

Lastly, if you are filing against a business—you don't want to get your claim thrown out if you lack the proper information—I suggest that you verify the proper name of the business; the proper name of the owner(s) of the business; and whether there is an attorney or agent that represents the business. This information is a public record and can generally be obtained from your state's Secretary of State's officer or some similar state entity.

Some states allow small claims to be filed by mail. If so, you should be sure to learn what the claim by mail rules are. As you might expect, small claims courts have a limit on the amount of damages that can be awarded to a successful plaintiff. In addition, small claims court filing fees typically are lower than for "regular" (higher damage limit) claims. For a list of state small claims courts limits, see **Appendix D.**

Alternate Dispute Resolution (ADR)

Many courts have been evolving from the adversarial system to the ADR, or Alternative Dispute Resolution system. Indeed, in some cases, if a lawsuit is filed, the courts might order mandatory ADR before the dispute gets moved forward through the system.

ADR takes two general forms: arbitration and mediation. In **arbitration**, a court-appointed or approve arbitrator meets with the opposing parties at one or more times, takes testimony, receives evidence, and thereafter renders a decision, usually in writing. Systems vary, but in many cases, the arbitrator's decision resolves the issue. In cases when it does not, the parties are then free to appeal to the court, but it is likely that the arbitrator's decision—after all, he or she is *court-appointed or approved*—will be given great weight by the reviewing court.

Mediation differs from arbitration because a mediator is likely to be more active in resolving the dispute.

Mediators usually act with more leeway than arbitrators, including separating the parties and holding individual conversations with them to resolve the issues at hand. It has been said that the mediator's job is getting the opposing parties to say "yes," with the goal that all parties walking away from the proceeding will have the view that they got much, if not all, of what they wanted.

Lawyers

But, "aha", you say. *"I'm not going to deal with this matter all alone, I will just hire a lawyer to do my work for me."* True, and as a lawyer, I would be the last person to advise you <u>not</u> to seek legal advice. Just remember, however, unless you just happen to have a relative or friend who will represent you for free, lawyers expect to be paid, usually with an upfront retainer. In addition, especially in small claims disputes, the cost of hiring a lawyer might not be worth it.

Hire a lawyer if you desire, but just make sure that when you do, you establish a mutual agreement on what your expectations are and what you are willing to pay for them. Lastly, remember that lawyers should be considered as "counselors", not just litigators. Often the advice you get from a competent attorney will not always result in you and your problem landing in court. Indeed, some lawyers might suggest some of the approaches I have written about earlier in this chapter.

Chapter II
Making Your Point

Create a List   pg. 20
Find the Right Party   pg. 21
Learn the Law   pg. 22
Talking to Your Other Neighbors   pg. 22
Approaching the Problem Neighbor pg. 23
Assemble the Necessary Documentation pg.25
Promptness pg.27
Appropriate Dress pg. 27
Staying Calm pg. 28
Practice Your Argument pg. 28

Create a List

I am a big fan of lists. I use them for several tasks, including shopping, traveling and planning projects, even writing this guidebook.

There is a saying that "preparation is everything." Bearing that saying in mind, it is important for you to make the proper preparations if you want to prevail in a neighbor-to-neighbor dispute. This principle holds true whether you come to an informal resolution of the problem, or ultimately wind up in court, or somewhere in between.

You would be surprised how many people have lost disputes despite the strength of their positions, simply because they could not back up their claims. Since you don't want to run into this kind of dilemma, especially if you intend to fight for your rights without legal representation, you need to prepare a checklist. A sample checklist appears below:

Dispute Resolution Checklist

- What is the precise nature of your dispute?
    What's the issue?
    How long has it been going on?

- What rules are being broken?
    State Law
    Local Ordinances
    HOA CC&Rs

> Deed Restrictions
> Surveys
> Other agreements

- Do I have copies of the necessary documents?
- If not, how do I get copies?

> Search personal files
> Deed records
> Websites
> Other sources

- Do I have any documentation of the problem?

> Written documents?
> Photographs?

- Have I approached the neighbor about resolving the problem?

- Have I talked to any officials?
  > HOA board officials
  > Public Officials
  > Polices
- Do I have any witnesses?
  > If so, are they willing to testify, or make a written statement?

Find the Right Party

If you are a residential property owner, you probably have a good idea of who owns the property next door to you. But this is not always the case. Perhaps your next-door neighbor is a renter, or is house-sitting for the owner. Additionally, in some cases, the owner could be a corporation or other some other kind of legal business entity.

In any case, if your dispute boils down to litigation, or some other procedure for resolving it, you should make sure that you are going up against the proper party. Usually a check of the deed records will provide this information. Sometimes, with corporate or other business entities, you should check with your Secretary of State's office.

Learn the Law

If you are going to complain about your neighbor's violation of the "rules," then you ought to know what those rules are.

If you hire a lawyer, then it will be the lawyer's job to review the appropriate rules. If you are going it alone, then you need to review the language of the appropriate state law or ordinance, HOA CC&R, or deed restriction on your own. If you feel uncomfortable about doing this, you could approach a trusted friend to assist you. If you're comfortable with the internet, there are several websites, such as www.USLegal.com, or FINDLAW.com, etc., that provide free information to consumers about various legal subjects.

Talking to Your Other Neighbors

While this is not always true, problems like fence disputes or falling trees usually only involve you and your neighbor. On the other hand, concerns about barking dogs and other loud noises, or inappropriate businesses, or nuisances, reach beyond your own property. In situations like that, you might want to approach your neighbors who also are suffering. Sometimes presenting a united front can be more effective than your sole complaint.

Approaching the Problem Neighbor

Talking with your neighbor usually is fine when you're discussing mundane things like the weather, or how your kids are doing in school. It can be a different matter, however, when the conversation to turns to matters of conflict such as loud noises, boundary disputes, fallen trees, etc. What do you do then?

Approaches to this problem differ, but there is a common theme of when dealing with this problem:

- **People tend to be territorial** so when you first try to deal with the problem, **try to pick a neutral meeting place**—not your home or your neighbor's. Try instead, if you can, a place like library, a neighborhood recreational center meeting room, the YMCA if you have one, maybe even the local golf course.
- **Visit your neighbor,** if you can't arrange a neutral meeting place. Part of the art of resolving conflict is creating a level of comfort for your adversary. Accordingly, it makes more sense for you to go to your neighbor's home, where he or she has a level of comfort that might not occur if you have the neighbor come to

your home first, where the neighbor may feel "summoned."

- **Soften your initial approach**. Sometimes the better course of action is to start the conversation about something that is indirectly related to the issue you want to discuss. Here is an example of what could be a starting point about a problem you are having:

[You]: Wow, the weather has been really horrible lately!

[Your neighbor]: That's for sure! My lights were out for about four hours, and some of my vegetable garden took a major hit. What about you?

[You]: I don't have your 'green thumb," so my vegetables didn't suffer as much. The back of my garage is a different story.

[Your neighbor]: Your garage? What happened?

[You]: Well... You know that big oak tree you have...?

Not an Oscar-winning script, but you probably get the idea. Sometimes, in times of potential neighbor conflict, it's best to engage in little "misdirection." The payoff might be your neighbor agreeing to cooperate to fix the problem rather than having the conversation escalate into something else.

- **Don't automatically think your neighbor is aware of the problem**. Contrary to what you might think, most people don't ordinarily fall straight out of bed armed with evil intentions. When you do approach your neighbor, do it with the idea that he or she is not necessarily aware of the issue.

- Based on the circumstances, **expect a neighbor complaint against you**. Neighborhood conflict is **not** a one-way street. If you do have a grievance against your neighbor for some reason or another, don't be surprised if he or she lodges some complaint against you. In anticipation of this, you should think about whether you might have been guilty of some kind of neighbor neglect in the past—fallen trees, a boisterous dog or cat, loud parties, etc.
- Once you get to speaking about the issue you are concerned about, remember to:

(1) **State the complaint**—what is your issue?

(2) **Present the law**—what is the complaint based on:

> State or local law.
> HOA CC&R
> Private agreement

Assemble the Necessary Documentation

Get the appropriate paperwork!

If your claim involves a covenant, condition, or restriction (CC&R), get a copy of it and be ready to produce it when it is necessary. In addition, make sure you understand the language you are relying on to prove your point.

Sometimes in the heat of emotion, we read what we want to read. Make sure you know what you're talking about. If your claim involves a local ordinance or state law, get a copy of the appropriate legislation and be ready to produce it when it is called for.

If a paper copy is not readily available, you should be able to visit your local government's website, download a copy of the necessary materials, and print them out for your use. If you have had correspondence, electronic or otherwise with your neighbor, or any person or entity regarding the issue at hand, be sure to have copies ready.

NOTE: If any previous written communications you have had on the issue (including email, tweets, etc.) contain strong language that is irrelevant to or deviates from the facts at issue, please be prepared to defend it, disavow it, or otherwise diminish its possible negative impact on your position. In addition, despite the annoying nature of the conflict between you and your neighbor, avoid using strong language in any future communications. Stick to the facts.

Sometimes your dispute with your neighbor will be about property boundaries. If a dispute is over an existing survey, get a copy of the survey. If you think you need a new survey to prove your point, contact a reputable surveyor (ask your real estate who they use, or talk to your neighbors, or your HOA officials) and get the new survey done.

If your dispute involves deed covenants, CC&Rs or other paperwork, (e.g., a written partition fence agreement), make sure you have a copy available, and be sure to review ahead of time it in case you are asked questions about it.

Promptness

Timing is everything. One of the worst things you can do is show up late for a hearing about your dispute (if it comes to that). If you do, the decision maker—perhaps a judge, magistrate or hearing office; perhaps an arbitrator or a mediator—will inherently believe that you are not serious about your claim and be subtly influenced to rule accordingly.

So, if you need to take public transportation get to the meeting, make sure you have a current bus or transit schedule. If you are driving, beware of traffic advisories, toll booths and the weather. If you are driving and need to park, be aware of parking fees, as well as the distance between the parking area and where you need to be.

Appropriate Dress

I am not asking you wear a tuxedo or a formal cutaway jacket, but you want to be taken seriously. In an ideal world, your clothing should not matter—but it does. Let's face it, showing up for a serious meeting in a tank top and cutoffs is not likely to elicit confidence. The same thing goes for excessive makeup, cleavage (male or female), piercings or tattoos. Despite your claims that you want to "be yourself," the primary issue in most neighborhood disputes involves property rights, not your individual self-expression.

Staying Calm

Don't get emotional. Stick to the facts at hand! Sometimes neighborhood disputes are more about emotions and long-held grudges then they are about the facts. The more emotional you get about your situation, the more likely you are to get off-track. If you have friends who can provide you with steady and *quiet* moral support, bring them. So, take a deep breath before you proceed, and let the facts speak for themselves.

Practice your argument

Lawyers role-play all the time. How many times have you watched a television show where a lawyer has set up a "mock jury" to practice his or her argument before the case comes to court?

You can do the same thing, but at a less formal level. If you are going to be representing yourself at a hearing about a neighborhood dispute, think about practicing your argument in front of a trustworthy friend. It can't hurt.

In sum, even if you have the strongest feelings that your cause is just, proper preparation will go a long way toward helping you prevail.

Chapter III

Noise Law Generally pg. 30
Anti-Noise Legislation pg. 31
State Anti-Noise Laws pg. 32

Local Anti-Noise Laws pg. 32

Noise Prohibitions in Rental Agreements pg. 33

Restrictive Covenants pg. 35

Remedies pg. 35

Approaching Your Neighbor pg. 35

Warning the Neighbor pg. 36

ADR (Mediation) pg. 37

Police Involvement pg. 37

Litigation (Suing for Nuisance) pg. 38

Questions and Answers pg. 39

Noise Law Generally

We all have heard the oft-quoted phrase, "Stop making a nuisance of yourself." Noise abatement laws primarily are based on the common law concept of "nuisance." The word "nuisance" has many definitions, but in legal terms is thought to be a person, thing, or activity that intrudes upon the lives or property of others without actually causing a physical trespass.

Nuisance laws developed out of the deficiencies of trespass law requiring a person to physically invade and cross over a neighbor's property line before there could be any liability for damages. Nuisance law tried to fill the void left by the inadequacies of trespass law when neighbors did not create actual trespass, but rather, did things like creating noxious fumes, dust, or just made too much of a disturbance, even if the activity did not constitute a "trespass" in the usual sense. Noise is probably at the top of the nuisance list.

Noise is always a factor in our lives, whether we live in a large community, in a rural area, or somewhere in between. Noise can come in many forms—car and truck traffic, loud conversations, the sound of railroads and airplanes, and the sounds created by manufacturing or farming. It varies in form and intensity, and our tolerance for noise can be traced to where we live as well as our relative distance from the noise.

Noise is a relative thing. The key to recognizing a noise problem and its possible resolution is context, including whether we are especially sensitive to what most people would consider to be ordinary sounds. For example, all dogs bark. The question is one of degree.

Anti-Noise Legislation

Noise legislation is usually targets an activity termed as a "public disturbance" or "disturbing the peace." Violations are usually classified as minor criminal offenses, particularly in residential areas, such as when a person operates a tool, equipment, vehicle, electronic device, machine, or any other noise or sound-producing devise. Public disturbances are generally distinguished from activities that only disturb a particular individual. Often they overlap, however, and the remedy is usually injunctive relief (legally forcing the activity to stop), or a suit for money damages.

Typical anti-noise legislation begins with a statement as follows: *"It is unlawful for any person to cause, or for any person in possession of property to allow to originate from the property, sound that is a public disturbance noise."* The statement is then followed by a listing of the sounds that are characterized as "public disturbance noises."

Some loud noises, however, are inevitable and generally incapable of being prohibited by anti-noise legislation. Some noises, because of combination of policy issues, or the impracticality of regulating them, are often excluded from the definition of a public disturbance. Excluded noises can include:

- Sounds caused by natural phenomena (e.g., waterfalls, thunder, lightning)
- Sounds from aircraft in flight
- Sounds that originate in airports that are directly related to flight operations
- Sounds created by firearms during lawful hunting activities
- Sounds created by railroads
- Sounds created by fire alarms, warning devices, bells, chimes, etc., that last for longer than a designated time (e.g., five minutes)
- Sounds coming from officially designated parades or public events
- Sounds created by equipment used in highway maintenance

This list is not exhaustive. You should consult your local laws to find out how they define prohibited noises.

State Anti-Noise Laws

Using nuisance law as a basis, most states have statutes that provide municipalities with the power to "prevent noise and disturbance."

Local Anti-Noise Laws

In addition to state law, many municipalities have enacted local anti-noise or noise control legislation. For example, the City of Shaker Heights, Ohio has a noise control ordinance that specifically defines a "noise disturbance" as any sound which:

- **Endangers or injures the safety or health of humans and animals;**
- **Annoys or disturbs a reasonable person of normal sensitivities; or**
- **Endangers or injures persons or real property.**

Some jurisdictions that regulate the noise level of certain activities have decibel machines that can be set up, if requested, to monitor the level of noise coming from your neighbor's property.

Local ordinances usually make a nuisance either a crime or a civil violation. If it is a crime—usually a misdemeanor—if found guilty, the perpetrator could be subject to fines, or possibly jail if he fails to appear in court if summoned. The city has the burden of prosecuting the nuisance, whether it is a civil or criminal violation of a city ordinance. As a complaining neighbor, your role is limited to testifying in court if the nuisance case goes to trial. Any fines collected for violation of the ordinance are awarded to the city, not you.

Noise Prohibitions in Rental Agreements

Noise abatement clauses in lease agreements fall under the general rule that tenants have a duty not to disturb the "quiet enjoyment" of their fellow tenants. To help cure this problem, it is standard practice for a lease agreement to contain a clause like the following:

"Tenant, and such tenant's visitors, shall not make or cause any improper noises in the building, nor interfere in any way with the use and enjoyment of other tenants and their respective premises."

Some lease agreements contain even more specific anti-noise clauses, such as the following examples:

"(1) Vocal or instrumental music shall not be permitted before [_____] a.m., or after [_____] p.m."

(2) Children shall not cause disturbances or create hazards in the common hallways, stairways, or elevators."

These kinds of anti-noise lease agreement clauses serve a two-fold purpose:

(1) They put tenants on notice that certain kinds of activities will not be tolerated and are prohibited; and

(2) if these activities occur, the landlord (or fellow tenants) can use this information to pursue an action for "breach of lease"—in the landlord's case as the basis for a possible eviction; in the tenant's case, as basis to vacate the premises, or serve as a vehicle for some kind of accommodation, perhaps even for a partial rent abatement.

The landlord's right to prohibit the playing of loud music, and similar noises, can be traced to three separate and distinct sources:

(1) The tenant's statutory or common law duty not to disturb any neighbor's peaceful enjoyment of their premises,
(2) The common law covenant of quiet enjoyment, which a landlord makes with the landlord's tenant, and

(3) Possible sanctions against the tenant for the violation of municipal anti-noise regulations and ordinances.

Restrictive Covenants

Restrictive covenant anti-noise clauses are like the types found in standard lease agreement clauses.

Remedies

There are a number of ways to deal with disturbing noises from your neighbors. Several, but not all, involve resorting to the legal system. The methods include direct involvement with your neighbor about the problem; warning the neighbor about the problem in some fashion, either personally or in writing; utilizing an impartial third-party—usually through mediation—to deal with and help resolve the problem; calling the police if the problem is extremely problematic; or, lastly, suing the neighbor—with the threat of damages—to end the offending behavior.

Approaching Your Neighbor

As I have mentioned before, a direct one-on-one approach with your neighbor has two sides—one good, one bad. If you get along with your neighbor in the first place, then a one-on-approach is probably a good thing. On the other hand, if your neighbor is constantly engaged in loud behavior, then a one-on-one approach probably won't work.

It is likely that a neighborhood noise problem is not limited to you alone; other residents in the neighborhood are likely experiencing the same problem. In this case, a group approach might be warranted—so long as everyone involved takes a pledge to remain calm!

Warning Your Neighbor

Assuming a one-on-one approach will not work, what's next? Here I think the most reasonable position is to send the neighbor a notice, using this suggested format:

Dear [Neighbor's name]

As you know, we have discussed the [describe the behavior], on previous occasions, and I/we have requested that you refrain from such behavior because it has become a continued annoyance to my family and to the rest of the neighborhood. You have chosen not to refrain from this kind of behavior.

Every property owner in this neighbor is subject to the same sets of rules regarding noise control. Your activities have been in direct violation of [state specific ordinance number, HOA rule, restrictive covenant, etc.].

We are once again requesting that you refrain from your continued behavior forthwith. If you do not do so, we will have no choice other than to pursue appropriate legal action.

Sincerely,

 [Signatures]

Alternative Dispute Resolution (ADR)

Sometimes the best route for resolving neighbor noise disputes is to utilize the services of a third party. For example, there are many companies that provide professional mediation services for HOAs. For example, a firm known as the ADR Center provides such services. It offers a Home Owners Association Mediation Program *"..designed to provide a time-efficient, convenient and confidential forum for the resolution of disputes involving Homeowners Associations. Disputes involving association rules and regulations, neighbor relations, construction defects, maintenance, common areas and fees and assessments are a few of the types of disputes appropriate for mediation."* Further information about the ADR Center can be found on their website at www.theadrcenter.org.

Police Involvement

Let's face it, some neighbors will simply be uncooperative. Whether it's a string of noisy parties, general raucous behavior, or the unsettling sound of racing car engines, or motorcycles specially equipped with loudspeakers one can hear hundreds of yards away, some people simply refuse to act in a civil, civilized manner.

In cases like this, your only avenue it to resort to calling the police. Even that action, however, should not approached lightly. In these kind of cases, before you call the authorities, you still need to:

- Document the offending behavior. A good idea would be to keep a written journal detailing times, dates, and type of

- incident. If appropriate, you also might want to have some
- digital videos or photographs. Modern smartphones can serve a useful purpose.
- Get the support of your neighbors. As I explained earlier, noise issues rarely affect one property owner alone.
- Encourage your neighbors by asking them to keep journals
- and recording videos, if possible.
- Visit your local police station before you make the call and make the authorities aware of the problems you are facing. Sometime a well-timed visit to the police station, followed by a police visit with the neighbors, might help soften the problem—especially if the neighbors learn that their behavior could possibly lead to fines or prosecution for a misdemeanor.

Litigation (Suing for Nuisance)

Suppose you have gone the civil violation or criminal misdemeanor route and you are still not satisfied? At this point, you have two basic options: (1) consider the matter closed, or (2) think about suing your neighbor for creating or allowing a nuisance.

Litigation is never easy. In this kind of situation, you have the burden of hiring a lawyer, or taking on the case alone, including paying for all filing fees, document duplication services, and travel expenses in getting though the court process

And remember one thing: ***Suing isn't winning and winning does not mean you get everything you want.***

If you sue to try to stop a nuisance, there are four basic elements you must show the courts in order for you to prevail:

- *The neighbor's actions seriously annoy you.*

Here you will have to demonstrate that you are a reasonable person and, accordingly not extra sensitive to the neighbor's actions. A good idea would be to have available copies of any correspondence with your neighbor showing your attempts to get him to cease or modify his behavior.

- *The neighbor's actions have reduced your ability to enjoy the peaceful enjoyment of your property.*
- *The neighbor is responsible for his actions, or the person who is causing the disturbance is acting on the neighbor's behalf or with his knowledge.*
- *Injunctive relief (getting the noise to cease), or a specific monetary amount will adequately compensate you for the neighbor's actions.*

NOTE: In accordance with legislation in some states, the neighbor's actions must be either "unreasonable" or "unlawful"

Questions and Answers

Q & A: I live in an apartment building. My neighbor has a dog that barks loudly at all hours. What should I do?

First, you might want to check with your landlord to find out if animals are allowed on the premises. If they are not, you probably should approach the landlord to let him know that (1) you are entitled to the peaceful enjoyment of your apartment; and (2) if dogs and other animals aren't allowed on the premises, then your fellow tenant could be in breach of his lease and the landlord should take action.

Keep in mind, however, that some of your neighbors, if they are disabled, may be entitled to own "service dogs" and other service animals, in accordance with local, state, or federal laws regarding "reasonable accommodations" for persons characterized as disabled.

Q & A: Suppose the landlord does allow dogs on the premises?

Even when dogs and other animals are allowed on the premises, even if they are "service dogs," your neighbor is not entitled to a blank check. He or she still has an obligation to respect your right to the quiet enjoyment of your leased premises. Your best bet here is to speak to your landlord about the situation and ask that he discuss the issue with your fellow tenant, perhaps suggesting some behavior training for the dog.

Q & A: My neighbors play loud music. What should I do?

Like dogs barking, the question here is a matter of degree. Does your neighbor play loud music all the time? Or does it happen only occasionally, such as at a birthday party or a holiday celebration? If the occurrences are very rare, then it's probably better for you to grin and bear it, or if you are able, leave the premises for a short time until the good times stop rolling. On the other hand, if the noise is persistent, then perhaps it is time to take up further action.

For example, let's assume you live in an apartment building and you have a consistently loud neighbor. Under most state or local laws, and often in their individual leases, residential tenants are required to respect the "peaceful" or "quiet" enjoyment of others. Usually this means that they are supposed to conduct themselves (as well as their friends) in a manner that does not unduly disturb their neighbors.

Your first option is to discuss the matter with your offending neighbor. If you are wary about doing that for a number of reasons—you and your neighbor don't get along, or you have had some previous unresolved issues with your neighbor—then the next step is to consult with your landlord and discuss the situation and its possible resolution.

Although highly unlikely, if it comes to that, you might even discuss the concept of "constructive eviction"; that is, the landlord's failure to remedy a condition (including regulating the noise of your fellow tenants), causing you to have no choice but to vacate the premises with no further liability for the payment of rent. The real-life problem with trying the constructive eviction route is that you have to move out, and when you do, you take the chance that you cannot prove your case after the fact. If this happens, you could be liable for unpaid rent.

All landlords are subject to implied warranties (promises) of quiet enjoyment for their tenants. While a tenant generally cannot assert as a breach of warranty the acts of third parties which are unauthorized by the landlord, it is possible that the playing of loud music by one tenant could occur with the tacit authorization of the landlord, thus subjecting the landlord to liability for breach of the implied warranty of quiet enjoyment. In addition, you might want to take a trip to city hall to ask whether the city has an anti-noise law in place.

Q & A: I live in a single-family house, not an apartment building. Like the apartment dweller, I still suffer from my next-door neighbor's refusal to stop playing loud music at all hours. I have already discussed the matter with him, to no avail. Any suggestions?

In many states, loud music is characterized as a nuisance under state law or local law. Some states, for example, define a "noise disturbance" as any sound which: "(1) Endangers or injures the safety or health of humans and animals; (2) Annoys or disturbs a reasonable person of normal sensitivities; or "(3) Endangers or injures personal or real property."[i]

Persons who violate local noise control laws can be subject to monetary fines or actual noise abatement. I would advise that you do some further research on the matter, and then discuss the proper course of action with appropriate city officials.

Q & A: What should I do when my neighbor starts his chainsaw or insists on mowing his lawn at 7 a.m. on a Sunday morning?

From your answer, I will assume that the use of the chainsaw is intermittent. Unless your neighbor has an unusual number of trees on his property, it is hard to fathom that a chainsaw would be in use that often. On the other hand, mowing the lawn at 7 a.m. on a Sunday morning seems a bit much. If it's habitual, I suggest that you approach your neighbor and see if a compromise can be achieved. If that doesn't work, consult your local noise ordinances, or your local HOA rules as appropriate.

Q & A: My neighbor's loud music is really getting to me. I have discussed the matter with him and he insists that it is "not that loud" and that I am "hyper-sensitive." Any suggestions for what I might do to solve this problem?

If talking won't help, you might think about investigating whether your HOA CC&Rs cover the subject of noise and what the remedies are.

If you're not a member of an HOA, then I suggest you consult with your local officials, or go to your city's website to find out what the local noise regulations are. Some cities regulate noise by decibel levels, and under the proper circumstances, will set up a decibel level measuring machine to determine if your complaints are justified.

Chapter IV
DOG LAW

Dog Law Generally pg.45

Local Dog Laws pg. 45

    At-Large Dogs & Impoundment pg. 46

    Dog Leashing and Control pg. 47

    Licenses pg. 48

    Disease Control pg. 48

    Control of Animal Waste pg. 48

    Dangerous Dog Ordinances pg. 48

    Questions and Answers pg. 49

Dog Law Generally

Most of us rarely are "on the fence" when it comes to animals, particularly domestic animals like dogs or cats. We either like them or we don't. How we and our neighbors deal with domestic animals continues to be a field ripe for any number of neighborhood disputes, usually involving excessive barking, animals running loose, biting, or failure to properly dispose of animal waste.

In addition to a body of local laws regarding the rights of property owners with respect to animals, there also is an ever-evolving body of law involving the rights of animals. For example, The Animal Legal Defense Fund (www.aldf.org) is an American non-profit law organization organized in 1979 to protect the rights and advance the interests of animals, particularly with respect to animal cruelty, through the legal system.

I acknowledge that dogs are not the only kinds of domestic animals that people own. Some people host a vast menagerie of animals including dogs, cats, snakes, monkeys, fish, birds, alligators—you name it. That being said, the overwhelming number of neighbor-to-neighbor disputes involving animals are dog-related. Accordingly, I will concentrate primarily on these kinds of issues.

Local Dog Laws

Local government rules and regulations regarding dogs and other domestic animals, usually take the form of some kind of ordinance. These ordinances involve a variety of subjects, including licensing, vaccination, leash laws, the number of dogs a person may keep on the premises, and procedures for impounding dogs and other animals. Some states even mandate, or require, local governments to enact ordinances for licensing of dogs or animal matters.

Local ordinances and state laws dealing with dogs attempt to strike a balance between protecting people and respecting dog owners' rights. Community's police powers are broad in dealing with dogs, in part because an owner can control only so much of a dog's behavior. Typical local dog ordinances cover the following:

- At-large dogs and Impoundment.
- Dog leasing and control
- Licenses
- Disease control
- Control of animal waste

At-Large Dogs & Impoundment

Dog impoundment is an extreme remedy for violations of dog leashing ordinances and is generally viewed as a last resort. Local authorities generally do not impound dogs immediately unless the dog is vicious, is an apparent health hazard, or is running loose with no apparent owner. In most other cases, the owner is first warned, and, thereafter fined. Unheeded repeated warnings and fines could lead to impoundment of the dog.

The subject of impounding dogs usually often is most controversial, as dog owners can face the potential loss of a beloved family pet. Dogs may be impounded under law for a variety of reasons. The most common reason a dog is impounded is because it is found running loose. Some states allow animal control officers to destroy loose dogs, especially if there is a concern whether the dog is dangerous or rabid.

Loose dogs can be impounded by a local dog pound, or an animal shelter will impound a dog for five to seven days after notifying its owner. If the owner does not retrieve his or her dog, the dog may then be placed for adoption, sold for research, or humanely euthanized.

Dog confinement laws concentrate on two primary issues:

- Secure confinement of the animal with a fence or other enclosure that will not allow the animal to escape.
- Accompanying the animal on a leash.

Dog Leashing and Control

Many communities have enacted dog leash laws that are designed (1) to inform dog owners that they cannot allow their dogs to run loose without a leash and (2) to provide for fines or impoundment of the dog if the dog leash laws are violated.

Dog Licenses

In most states, it is mandatory for your dog to be licensed. License fees vary, and licenses are generally renewable on an annual basis. Dog licenses are required to be attached to the dog at all times. Failure to have the dog licensed can lead to fines, and if the owner cannot be found, possible impoundment.

Disease Control

Property owners who do not have their animals properly vaccinated can be charged with a misdemeanor and are subject to fines, perhaps leading to impoundment of the dog.

Control of Animal Waste

Local control of animal waste ordinances focuses on two primary issues: disposal of animal waste on the owner's own premises, and disposal of animal waste while the owner is on public or private property other than his own.

In the first category, failure to provide for the proper disposal of waste can lead to violations of your area's nuisance laws, leading to fines and possible jail terms. The second category is generally aimed at people who allow their dogs (leashed or unleashed) to defecate on public or private property without bagging the waste.

Dangerous Dog Ordinances

Some jurisdictions have enacted so-called "dangerous dog ordinances," particularly directed at variations of the pit bull breed. Under these breed-specific laws, dogs such as pit bull breeds either have been banned altogether, or declared as vicious. Violations of these kinds of laws have led to substantial penalties. For a commentary on the potential costs of dog bites, see **Appendix E.**

Questions & Answers

Q & A: **My neighbor's dog barks all night. What should I do?** By your question, I assume the dog is left outside at night. If you are already on decent terms, I suggest you approach her to find out what can be done. If you don't know the neighbor, or you feel uncomfortable about speaking with her, perhaps you could consult with your other neighbors, who I presume might be suffering the same discomfort. If they also are bothered by barking, perhaps the neighbor who has the best rapport with the dog owner could approach her to discuss the situation. Failing that, you might want to consult with your local officials.

Q & A: **Do these rules and approaches also apply to cats?**

Yes. The same rules apply whether the noise is coming from dogs, cats, birds, or some other domestic animal.

Q & A: **My neighbor is going out of town and wants me to feed and walk her dogs. What should I do?**

It depends. By your question, I assume you and your

neighbor get along, and thus she feels comfortable with you feeding and walking her dogs.

How large are the dogs? Are they trained? If they get sick, what are you supposed to do? Suppose the dogs bite or otherwise injure you, or a third party, particularly a child.

All of these issues need to be considered before you assume responsibility for your neighbor's dogs. Your best bet under these circumstances might be to suggest that she take her dog to a professional dog-sitting service.

Q & A: **I just held a birthday party for my granddaughter. In the excitement, my dog bit her. Now my daughter-in-law (whom I never liked) is threatening to sue me. What should I do?**

First things first. If the dog bit your granddaughter I assume you stand ready to pay for any medical bills, and if necessary, any counseling services your granddaughter might need as a result of the attack. Further, you probably ought to sit down with your daughter-in-law and your son so that this matter can be resolved before its gets out of hand and lands in the courts.

Q & A: **My neighbor's dog is always entering my yard. What should I do?**

In the first place, the general rule is that the owner of a domestic animal is responsible for any damage the dog does, no matter how the dog enters your property; whether it's crossing over your property line, jumping over the fence, burrowing, or any other way. In short, your neighbor is responsible for whatever damage the dog does to your property, regardless of whether the dog is vicious, or whether the dog's owner knows about the dog's propensity to enter the property of others.

In the meantime, while liability is clear, it seems to me that you are looking for immediate help. How does the dog get into your yard? Do you have a fence? If not, I suggest you think about getting one. If the fence is a boundary fence, and the dog burrows under it, you should plug the hole on your side of the property line and ask your neighbor to do the same on her side. If the fence is a boundary fence, and its condition is causing the dog to enter your yard, then your neighbor is responsible for maintaining and keeping his or share of the fence in good repair.

If you have fence with a defective latch and somehow the dog is getting into your yard because of it, you need to fix the latch. Lastly, do you have anything in your yard, i.e., a garden or something else that might be attracting the dog? If so, you should think about modifying it, or eliminating it. If all else fails, find out whether your neighbor has a dog lease that could be used, or whether your neighbor has ever purchased an "Invisible Fence" product. If not, perhaps you should suggest it.

Q & A: **We have a custom in this neighborhood that we must pick up our dog's poop. One of the new people on the block walks his dog daily, and the dog seems to put a "daily deposit" on my lawn. What should I do?**

There are a couple of ways to approach this problem. Rather than directly confronting your neighbor, I suggest getting one of those inexpensive "PUP" signs ("Pick Up Dog's Poop") and placing it prominently on your front lawn. In addition, if your neighbor has a regular dog walking routine, you might want to think about conveniently doing some "yard work" while your neighbor is passing by. Hopefully, your neighbor will get the point.

Q &A: My next-door neighbor has three dogs. Every other day the dogs defecate on her open patio in the back yard, and he doesn't clean up the mess for weeks at the time. Our yards are close together, and this creates quite a stench. What should I do?

You are describing a person who is either careless or doesn't care about health and safety. Waste not only smells, but also can attract all manner of flies and other insects. In most states, allowing the accumulation of feces can lead to fines. For example, in Seattle, Washington, such failures warrant a fine of $109 for each offense. While I usually recommend speaking with directly with your neighbor, for this issue you might want to go directly to the public health officials in your area and let them know about the situation.

Q & A: I have a well-behaved dog who does not like the feel of a leash. We have a nearby neighborhood park where I take my dogs for walks. The posted sign reads, "All dogs should be leashed." If I don't comply with the law, do I have any liability?

Of course, you do. That sign has been put up for a reason. Even a "well-behaved" dog is not immune from being spooked by other animals, or other people. There are many reasons to obey local leash laws, including:

- It's the law.

- Your dog is must less likely to cause harm or injury if it is under your control.

- All dogs—and their owners-- are not friendly.

- Physical abilities vary--not everyone you meet on the trail is physically able to withstand a dog jumping on them, even a so-called "nice dog."

- All your neighbors have the right to walk in a public park without being confronted by your loose dog.

Failure to abide by leash laws can have consequences, including fines. For example, violations of the Charlotte, North Carolina leash law could result in fines ranging from $50 for the first violation to up to a $500 fine, a citation, and permanent seizure of the animal for a fifth violation.

Q & A: I have two dogs, but I don't have licenses for them. The city where I live has a dog licensing law, but I just haven't gotten around to paying for the licenses. When I'm not walking them on leashes, I keep my dogs confined in my fenced-in backyard. Under these circumstances, I don't see the point purchasing dog licenses for them. Your thoughts?

Dogs have been known to break their leashes and escape from fenced-in yards. You should probably get licenses for both of your dogs for at least one or more of the following reasons:

- As I have mentioned before, it's the law in many jurisdictions, including yours. If you get caught with an unlicensed dog, you could get hit with a healthy fine. Do you want to risk that, especially since you have two unlicensed dogs?

- The cost of a dog license is probably far less than the cost of a fine for keeping an unlicensed dog.

Check your jurisdiction for the cost of dog licenses. You will probably be surprised about how inexpensive they are.

- If your dogs go missing, having licenses on them will probably improve your chances of getting them back.
- Licenses often provide your dog with a vaccination record. Dogs usually can't get licenses unless their vaccination records are up to date. If someone finds your dog, having an updated license will make it more likely that they will be willing to care for the dog until you are located.
- Some jurisdictions use a portion of their license fees to help support animal shelter efforts.

Q & A: I live in an apartment building. My new neighbor has moved in with a dog. I thought my building was "pet-free." Should I approach the landlord, or the new tenant about this?

Approach the landlord, not the tenant. Be aware, however, that under federal fair housing law, and some state laws, it is permissible, even in a "pet-free" building for persons with some disabilities to have a service dog as a reasonable accommodation for their disability. Keep in mind, that owning a service dog does not exempt the disabled person from their duty to refrain from engaging in activities that interfere with their neighbor's quiet enjoyment of the premises.

Q & A: **I live in an apartment complex. The complex has a designated dog run that is not used by my neighbor's dog. Instead, he allows the dog to defecate throughout the grounds. What should I do?**

Go directly to the landlord to report this violation. Your landlord is responsible for enforcing these kinds of rules.

Q & A: **I have a dog that I keep leashed in my yard. My dog is somewhat timid and somehow, I suspect that my neighbor's children are coming over into my yard from time to time to pet it or feed it. I am concerned that I might be responsible if the dog ever bites one of the kids. What should I do?**

In the first place, if the neighborhood children are coming into your yard without your permission, they are trespassing. You should inform their parents or guardians and ask them to contr0l their children's activities. Keep in mind, however, unless your dog is "vicious"—it doesn't seem so from its description—you are not ordinarily liable for injuries done by an animal when the injury occurred in a place where the dog has the right to be (your yard).

Q & A: **I am an electrician. Recently, while I was on a routine house call, I was confronted by the**

homeowner's large dog. Thankfully, before the dog could get too close to me, the homeowner got control of it, and took the dog outside, remarking that his pet was just "playful." Needless to say, I was not happy about the situation. In my business, I have confronted this kind of situation before. **What should I do in the future?**

As a practical matter in the future, you probably ought to think about asking any new clients whether they have animals and what kinds. If they answer that they own pets, especially large dogs, then you should let them know that you expect their dogs to be secured upon your next arrival for business. If not, you should think about dropping them as clients.

Speaking of business, your activities make you a "business visitor" and, as such, most dog bite statutes subject property owners to absolute liability if you are bitten or otherwise injured by their dog while you are conducting business.

An Arizona dog bite statute is a typical one relating to this kind of situation:

> "The owner of a dog which bites a person when the person is in or on a public place or lawfully in or on a private place, including the property of the owner of the dog, is liable for damages suffered by the person bitten, regardless of the former viciousness of the dog or the owner's knowledge of its viciousness."

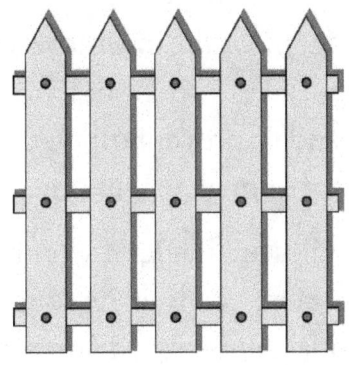

Chapter V
FENCES

Fence Law Basics pg. 58

Construction and Maintenance pg. 59

Partition or Division Fences pg. 60

    Partition Fence Agreements pg. 60

Fence Removal or Destruction pg.60

Statutory Fence Law pg. 61

Questions and Answers pg. 62

Fence Law Basics

Fences are enclosing structures around a yard or other space, and are intended to prevent "intrusion from without" or "straying from within" a building, or both. In simple terms, fences generally serve two purposes: to keep others out of your yard unless you permit them to enter, and to prevent others straying outside of your yard--usually children or animals—without your permission.

Most urban fences are made of wood, metal, brick, or some form of concrete. For fairly obvious reasons, barbed wire is rarely used in typical residential settings. In some areas, hedge or "live" fences are the norm.

Ordinarily, there are usually two kinds of fences: partition or division fences; or exterior fences. A partition or division fence is erected on the dividing line between the property of adjacent owners and serves as boundaries between the two parcels. As such, each of the adjacent owners may make use of the fence as part of his or her enclosure.

Under some state laws, property owners have a general duty to maintain a partition fence in equal shares. When conflicts occur about the maintenance of partition fences, the interpretation of the term, "equal shares" can sometimes be problematic. Further, a property owner generally may not eliminate a partition fence on his own without the consent of the adjoining property owner.

In residential areas, it is common for local rules to restrict the height of either constructed fences, or natural fences—bushes or trees. Local rules vary, but backyard fence height restrictions are not as strict as front yard fence restrictions. Backyard fence heights are typically limited to no more than six feet; front yard fences are typically limited to no more than four feet.

In some jurisdictions, such as Iowa and Massachusetts, fence disputes can be decided by certain township trustees known as "fence viewers", who have the power to determine fence-related controversies that arise under their state laws. For example, under Chapter 49, Section 14 of the Massachusetts General Laws, in cases of boundary disputes:

"If the division line between lands of respective occupants is in dispute or unknown, the fence viewers may designate a line on which the fence shall be built, and may employ a surveyor therefore; and such line shall, for the purpose of maintaining a fence, be deemed the division line between such lands until it is determined that the true line is in another place, and until so determined all laws relative to the erection, maintenance and protection of the fences shall be applicable to the fence erected or to be erected on such line."

Construction and Maintenance

Modern fence laws did not develop because people wanted keep their neighbors off their property. Instead, fence law evolved from the law's eventual recognition that farmers had a duty to fence in their animals, usually horses or cattle, to keep them from running at large into their neighbors' property. In most rural areas today, owners of adjoining properties are required to build, keep, and maintain their partition fences in good repair, unless the parties have agreed otherwise.

In modern law, where there is no general duty to construct a fence in a residential area, once constructed, the owner of the fence has a duty to maintain it. Further, if the owner of the fence has domestic animals, usually dogs, he has a legal duty to keep them from running at large.

Partition or Division Fences

Partition or division fences are fences that run along a common boundary between adjoining properties.

Partition Fence Agreements

Once the location of a partition fence has been determined, there are generally three ways to establish it: (a) by a written agreement between the adjoining owners; (b) by adverse possession or prescription, or (c) by statute. Some jurisdictions, usually in rural areas, can have additional local rules for resolving fence disputes including providing for informal agreements adjacent landowners may agree on the maintenance of a building or the maintenance of a partition fence.

If you and your neighbor want to enter into a formal understanding about your partition fence, you should always consider consulting a lawyer before entering into any legally-binding agreement. For an example of a Partition Fence Agreement, see **Appendix F**.

Fence Removal & Destruction

There is no prohibition against your removing or destroying a fence **on your own property**. On the other hand, removing your neighbor's fence or removing a common partition fence without your neighbor's consent subjects you to liability for damages and possible injunctive relief to force you to repair or replace the fence.

Statutory Fence Law

Some states have established partition fence laws. Minnesota law, for example, "requires neighboring owners or occupants of 'improved and used' land to contribute in equal shares to the cost of building and maintaining a partition fence between their lands if either owner wants to fence the land. This law is administered by 'fence viewers', local officials designated by the law." Other states have established similar partition fence laws.

In property law, a permanent fence is generally considered part of the land, and, in a sense, is to be considered a "building."

A property owner has a duty to keep his animals off the land of other persons. Subject to statutory provisions regarding fencing, a property owner has the right to have his land fenced, or unfenced. In addition, despite the feelings of his neighbors, a property owner may build fences on his property wherever he likes. In other words, most state laws do not prohibit the so-called "spite fence," even if the fence obstructs the neighbor's lights or interferes with sunlight. The law in most states is that a person's mean-spirited selfishness in constructing such a fence is irrelevant. Sometimes spite fences are referred to as "of-fence-ive" fences. Even though the law may be in your favor, if you want to build a spite fence just to vex your neighbor, you should be aware that your actions could result in a lawsuit costing you money, time, and in most cases, granting you no relief. Even if you win, you lose the money you spent.

Questions and Answers

Q & A: I went to an outdoor party at my neighbor's house yesterday. He has painted his side of our partition fence a horrible color. Can he do that?

Probably. It has been said that one man's trash is another man's treasure. And there is no accounting for taste. First you must note that you said the he painted "his side" of the partition fence. Generally, a property owner is free to do whatever he wants within his property line, especially if what he is doing doesn't affect the *exterior* of his property. If the paint job is that bad, unless your neighbor's property is covered by some kind of HOA governing how he paints the inside of his fence (I doubt it), I suggest that you grin and bear it. Failing that, based on how well you get along with your neighbor, maybe you could gently suggest another color.

Q & A: Because he has had some problems with deer entering his yard and devouring his garden vegetables, my neighbor wants to put up a barbed-wired fence. Is that legal?

Barbed wires are not inherently illegal, but unless you live in rural or semi-rural area, the type of fence you describe could be banned in your area. I would check your HOA rules if you have them, or consult with the city attorney's office, or someone from the zoning board. In addition, you might do some research on alternative fencing that could possibly solve your neighbor's problem.

For example, Dr. Leonard Perry of the University of Vermont suggests several ways to deal with deer, including:

- Building eight-foot high fences (especially useful against white-tailed deer). Fences that high, however, might violate local laws in your area.
- Building a six-foot high fence, but at a 45-degree angle, slanted outward. Such a fence, however, could be unsightly.
- Building one standard four-foot high fence and then placing another one about four feet away. According to Dr. Perry, if you use this arrangement, deer might not try to clear both fences and could perhaps get caught between them.
- Building a solid wood fence, or one with overlapping slats that deer cannot see through. These kinds of fences might be effective because the deer can't tell what is on the other side.
- Using a commercial-weight deer netting if the deer pressure is low or moderate. These kinds of products are easier to work with than wire mesh, and less expensive and blend into the landscape.
- Stringing single strands of monofilament twine between fence posts, about six inches apart.
- Using electric fences. I don't recommend these, especially if children might have a chance of getting injured. In addition, these kinds of fences could be prohibited in your area.

Q & A: My neighbor and I have a wooden partition fence. He wants to tear it down and create a hedge or "live" fence? I like the partition fence as it is. What should I do?

Tearing the partition fence down requires mutual consent. Do you two have a Partition Fence Agreement in place?

If so, you should review it. If you can't find it, keep in mind that there may be an existing agreement in place and already filed at the appropriate county recorder's office. If you don't have an agreement, then you should consider establishing one.

As for the hedge fence, if you don't you want one, perhaps you and your neighbor should discuss some sort of compromise.

Q & A: **My neighbor does a poor job of controlling the weeds and brush in his yard and it's quite unsightly. He used to keep his property in immaculate condition, but now he is getting on in years and I am not sure how I should approach him about this problem. His home is next to mine and I am thinking of selling my home in a few years. I know potential buyers would be put off by what they see next door. What should I do?**

Most cities have regulations regarding property owners' responsibilities to cut, trim, and remove weed and brush. Failure to do so can often result in substantial fines based on the length and severity of the offense. In your situation, you have at least a couple of reasonable options.

First, you might want to check in on your neighbor. Perhaps he is ill and needs medical attention. If, as you said, he used to keep his property in top shape it is likely that he is distressed as you are about his yard's appearance. After speaking with him, perhaps you can suggest a reasonably priced landscaping service. In addition, in some jurisdictions, some landscaping services are provided for the elderly by city personnel for a modest fee. Lastly, based upon your own physical condition, and that of your children, perhaps you might consider helping him out with his yard work from time to time. Or, at least until you are ready sell your property.

Q & A: I had an agreement with my former neighbor to maintain our wooden partition fence. He sold his house about six months ago, and a few patches of rough, rainy weather have severely damaged the fence. I want to have the fence repaired, but now my new neighbor is balking at the potential costs. What should I do?

I assume your agreement was in writing. If so, and if it was drafted properly, successive property owners would generally be required to honor its terms, including the costs. I suggest you review the agreement and then consult with your neighbor.

Q & A: My neighbor and I have mutually agreed to erect a partition fence and share the costs. What do we need to do?

Take a look at the Partition Agreement Form in **Appendix F**, and consider adapting it to your needs.

Q & A: My neighbor wants to build a 10-foot-high fence around his backyard. I think it's going to look hideous. Can he do that?

A ten-foot fence seems high, but it all depends on where you live. Most urban communities have local ordinances that prohibit fences from being over a certain height, so it is highly likely that your local ordinances or HOA rules, if any, disallow fences of over a certain height. A six-foot-high maximum seems to be standard.

An ordinance allowing a fence over eight feet in a residential area would be highly unusual. Check your local fence rules.

Q & A: My neighbor's lot sits on high ground to my immediate east. He has indicated he may be building a new fence which would block the view from my kitchen window where I like to have coffee in the morning and watch the sunrise. I think he's building the fence out of pure spite because of a property line dispute we had years ago. I know he has the right to fence his yard, but aren't spite fences illegal?

Actually, they're not. In Ohio, for example, no one has a prescriptive right over light and air. Therefore, even if your neighbor's fence is being erected for a malicious reason, even though it serves no useful or ornamental purpose, in most states you have no legal right to stop him.

Perhaps your best course is to try to calmly reason with your neighbor to stop him from erecting the fence. If your neighbor persists, you should first check to find out whether you live in a state that frowns upon spite fences. Or whether your local HOA, if any, forbids what he wants to do. If so, you might have a fair shot if you threaten him with litigation if decides to construct the fence.

Q & A: Two new neighbors have moved next door and they have has brought two large, rambunctious dogs with them. Unfortunately, the lot next door has no fence. The dogs are always breaking loose from their leashes and getting into my flower garden. I asked the neighbors to either get rid of the dogs, get stronger leashes, or fence them in. They refuse on all counts. What can I do?

Since you have indicated that persuasion isn't working, you have a number of possibilities. Most state laws provide that owners of domestic animals are not allowed to let them run at large. In addition, it is likely that you have local ordinances that prohibit this kind activity. In addition, in your case, local HOA rules might be in effect.

For example, an Austin, Texas dog control ordinance reads, in part, that "a person may not restrain a dog in a manner that allows the dog to move outside the person's property." Further, if you live in a condominium community, you might want to consult the rules and regulations of your condominium association. Lastly, you might want to think about simply fencing in your garden, or perhaps suggest to your neighbors that they purchase a product like "Invisible Fence."

Q& A: Could I use barbed wire?

That is probably not a good idea. It is likely that local law would prohibit the use you propose. Even where permissible, in most cases you would need the written consent of your neighbor, which you're not likely to get. The simple reason for it not being a good idea is that something, perhaps a dog or another animal, or someone, perhaps a child, will get hurt. The liability—and bad PR—from an injury like that just is not worth it.

Q & A: I have purchased an older home that has a brick fence running along a common boundary. Lately, bits of the fence have started to crumble and my neighbor is pestering me about repairing it. Because of the expense involved, I am inclined to simply tear it down. Can I do that without getting into trouble?

You should check your deed (or other deeds the "chain of title"). If any of them contains a covenant ("promise") that the property owner must maintain the fence as originally constructed, you may have to continue to maintain it "as is," or face legal action from your neighbor if you fail to do so. It is likely, especially with the age of the home and the passage of time, that you and your neighbor will be able to reach a reasonable compromise about the management and upkeep of the fence.

Q & A: There is a fence that runs right down the property line of my residence and that of my neighbors. Who has to maintain it?

Unless you have some written agreement that states otherwise, both of you have equal duties to maintain the fence in good repair.

Q & A: I have a fence on my own land that I have allowed by neighbor to connect to at the back corner of my backyard so that she can maintain a small vegetable garden. I want to tear my fence down and replace with a new one. Between the time I have the fence torn down and replaced with a new one, I know some of the neighbor children will use the opening as a short cut. possibly damaging the garden. Since this is not "partition fence" situation, however, do I have to get my neighbor's permission to tear down my fence?

Ordinarily, the rule is that you may remove any portion of a fence constructed entirely on your own property. In this case, however, you and your neighbor obviously have at least some implicit agreement that the fence will help protect his garden.

Under these circumstances, the general rule is that you should not remove the fence without giving your neighbor reasonable notice so he can take adequate steps to protect his garden.

Chapter VI
Adjoining Landowners

Adjoining Landowners Generally pg. 71

Boundaries pg. 71

Permissible Uses of Property pg. 73

Trees, Branches, and Roots pg. 74

Other Encroachments pg. 75

Lateral and Subjacent Support pg. 75

Prohibitions Against Storage of Dangerous Substances pg. 76

Easements for Light, Air and View pg. 76

Avoiding Dangers to Your Neighbors pg. 78

Questions and Answers pg. 79

Adjoining Landowners Generally

In addition to fence boundary, maintain and repair issues, adjoining landowners must deal with several other mutual rights, duties and liabilities arising from the fact that their lands are contiguous. These issues include which activities are permissible on your property and your neighbor's property and which are not; the potential liability for damages caused by falling trees and branches, or problems caused by tree roots; other encroachments; duties to provide lateral and subjacent support; prohibition against the storage of dangerous substances on your property; and easements for light, air, and view.

The term "adjoining landowners" means the owners of lands that are separated by a common boundary. The generally accepted common law rule is that every person may make such use as he or she will of his or her own property, so long as the person uses it in such a manner as not to injure the rights of others, and the use does not cause a nuisance. This is not a hard and fast rule, however, and is not meant to be applied in all circumstances. One is entitled to make "reasonable use" of one's property and the test for whether the use is reasonable depends on whether the owner has regard for all interests affected, his or her own, as well as those of his or her neighbors.

Boundaries

The real property that you own or occupy is said to be your "territory." In plain English, a "boundary" is the marking or dividing line between two separate parcels of land, or territories.

Boundaries in most urban residential areas are determined by surveyors, described in deeds and other conveyance instruments, and marked by partition or division fences. In other cases, where there are no boundary fences, boundaries are simply the "invisible lines" that separate your land from that of your neighbor's, often determined by reference to your yard or a driveway, or both. If water, such as a river or stream, separates your properties, the general rule is that the boundary is considered to be the middle of the bed of the river or stream.

Sometimes boundaries are determined by "acquiescence;" that is, they arise when adjacent landowners have recognized where the alleged boundary is for a certain number of years, and they agree on a boundary for convenience and treat it as the true boundary.

Other boundaries are determined by "prescription" as opposed to "acquiescence." Prescription is substantially similar to acquiescence and usually arises when, on adjacent property, it is known where the true, surveyed boundary is and the actual fence is not on the boundary, but the owners continue to use the fence as a boundary, creating a so-called "easement by prescription."

Boundaries can also be secured by the use of a doctrine called "adverse possession." As you might imagine, adverse possession situations often involve lawsuits and generally arise when there is a much more contentious relationship between the parties than there is with situations involving acquiescence or prescription.

Adverse possession starts out as a technical trespass upon the land of another, and requires the occupation of the land as a true owner would, for a specified period of time.

State laws vary on how one can obtain ownership of property using adverse possession. For a listing of the various state laws regarding adverse possession, including their statutes of limitation, see **Appendix G.**

The laws surrounding adverse possession are based on the point of view that a landowner should not "sleep on his rights." This is another way of saying that simply having title to property is not enough is not enough to own it. Accordingly, in order to maintain your property rights, you must be vigilant. If you are not, whether this seems logical to a layperson or not, a "trespasser" who acts like a "true owner" over a period of time can supplant the rights of the true owner!

Few fence disputes involving adverse possession play out in most modern residential communities, but they sometimes do occur.

Permissible Uses of Property

It is rare that a property owner, especially in a residential neighborhood, has the right to do whatever he or she wants to do on their land. A combination of zoning laws and private deed restrictions protect other property owners from their neighbors making "unreasonable uses" of their property.

What is "reasonable" will vary from state to state, and, sometimes, from region to region. For example, in some states, under some circumstances it is permissible to raise small cattle or poultry in an otherwise residential neighborhood. Some property owners do this for the extra income; some do it because some states provide property tax breaks for this kind of activity.

Trees, Branches, and Roots

Trees often act as boundaries between you and your neighbor's yard. You would be surprised how many people regularly fight over tree issues, usually involving boundaries, overhanging limbs and branches, or damages caused by falling trees and branches, and encroaching tree roots. What are the rules that guide us with respect to resolving these kinds of tree-related issues?

The first rule you should be aware of is that if a tree is standing on the division or boundary line between your property and your adjoining landowner's, so that the boundary line passes through the trunk or body of the tree, the tree is viewed as common property of both landowners as "tenants in common."

Being a tenant in common with your neighbor simply means that you are mutual owners of the property in question. In practical terms, as a tenant in common of a boundary tree, you and your neighbor have all shared rights and liabilities associated with the tree.

If a tree is not a boundary tree, then its ownership is based on where the trunk or body of it is located, not by the branches above, or the roots beneath it.

As for tree roots, most states take the position that if an adjoining landowner's tree roots damage your property, such as, for example, your home's foundation, the landowner is not liable to you. A few courts have held the landowner responsible for cutting back the offending tree roots.

Most courts, however, take the position that as a landowner, you have the right to cut back tree roots that are damaging your property, but that if you don't proceed carefully, you might be liable of the tree you are cutting is damaged.

Other Encroachments

Unless you and your adjoining property owner have come to some agreement, perhaps an easement, neither of you has the right to erect any buildings or other structures so that any part, no matter how small, extends beyond your individual property boundary lines.

Lateral and Subjacent Support

The right of lateral support is the right to which the soil in its so-called "natural state" must have support from adjoining land. The burden of providing lateral support is one of continued support running against the servient land (your neighbor's). In plain English, this means that your next door neighbor has a duty not do anything to his adjoining land that would have the effect of causing your soil to erode or otherwise slip away. The general rule is that even if the excavating owner acts diligently and with care, he cannot escape liability for removing lateral support to your land.

The right to subjacent support is related to lateral support, but it seldom relates to residential property owners' right; issues of subjacent support primarily relate to instances where an owner sells underlying mineral rights to his or her property, but retains ownership of the surface soil. In cases like that, if the acts of below-surface mining, even if done professionally and carefully, cause the surface soil to sink or be otherwise undermined, the miner could be liable for damages.

Common rights of lateral support only apply to land, not buildings. In many states, the common law rule has been modified by statute so that the right of lateral support, with some exceptions, also applies to buildings.

Prohibitions Against Storage of Dangerous Substances

As with other uses, zoning laws and CC&Rs most likely prohibit a property owner—at least a residential property owner—from storing any dangerous or explosive substances on the property. Anyone who does so is liable for all injuries to any adjoining or surrounding property which are the "natural and proximate result" of the explosion of such substances.

Easements for Light, Air & View

An easement is defined as an interest in land that grants or limits the right to use land by someone who does not own the land or possesses it. A simple example is you allowing your neighbor to cut through your backyard so that she can obtain a quicker and more efficient route to a bus or light rail stop. Like many of our laws, the rules governing a homeowner's "rights" to light, air, and view, are rooted in the common law of easements. Thus, under the English doctrine of "Ancient Lights", if a landowner had received sunlight across adjoining property for a specified period of time, he was entitled to continue to receive unobstructed access to such sunlight without limit.

This rule provided the benefited property owner was with a "negative prescriptive easement" and the owner could prevent the adjoining from obstructing his or her access to light with any structure, including a wall, a fence, a building, or any like structure. A "negative prescriptive easement" essentially is an interest in land that has evolved over time and allows you prohibit your neighbor from doing something on his own land that he would otherwise be able to do, such as have the right to block out your sunlight by building a high fence or other structure.

The rule of "Ancient Lights" once may have worked in medieval England, but recognizing its limitations in combination with modern urban living, this doctrine has largely been repudiated in the majority of U.S. jurisdictions.

Accordingly, if even if you have been enjoying your solar panels, or your unobstructed views, including those from your terrace, or your patio, if your neighbor decides to put up a fence or other structure that blocks your view, there is little you can do about it. Like with the "spite fence," your neighbor's motives, for good or ill, are irrelevant. Some HOA rules may address this issue.

In legal terms, if a covenant or agreement for light, air, and view benefits the land to which it relates and enhances its value, then the easement created becomes appurtenant to the land and passes with it.

In simple language, a deed, covenant, or other agreement which purports to reserve an easement of light and air in the premises granted runs *with the land* and **binds subsequent grantees of the premises.**

For an example of an Express Easement Agreement for Light, Air, & View, **see Appendix H.**

Avoiding Dangers to Your Neighbors

Sometimes conflicts with your neighbors have nothing to do with boundary disputes, or fallen trees, or too much noise. Sometimes neighborhood conflicts can arise even when you have the best of intentions.

For example, suppose you invite your next-door neighbor to visit you. People do that all the time. But since you have invited her, she should have a reasonable expectation that she should be able to enter your home without fear of injury. Accordingly, you have established a **duty** to your neighbor when you invite her to visit you.

Assume further that you have young children and they have been playing with marbles on your shiny hardwood floor in the foyer of your home leading to your front door. This scenario may seem far-fetched in today's world of social media, but some children still actually play with marbles.

So, you have observed your children playing with the marbles, and you know that your neighbor is on the way, but you get involved with other things and you forget to have your children put the marbles away before your guest arrives.

You neighbor rings your doorbell. You yell at her to "come on in." She enters your home, immediately slips on the marbles, falls, and injures her back. Now you have an **injury** resulting from your failure to observe your duty of care toward your neighbor—at least from your neighbor's lawyer's point of view.

The resultant injury causes your neighbor much "pain and suffering." That translates into **damages**. The same result could occur if your dog bites your neighbor causing injury. And, of course, there are always possibilities for injuries when children are involved.

Questions and Answers

Q & A: My neighbor has just had a large storage shed constructed next door. It is size of a small barn! I am certain that this structure violates the CC&Rs of my HOA. He has told me he got the proper permits before construction began but I don't believe. What should I do?

You might be right, but there are ways to be sure. Getting the "proper permits" may only mean that your neighbor got a construction permit from the city or other local government. These kinds of permits, however, do not trump your local HOA CC&RS. Consequently, you should review your HOA CC&Rs, or go to the HOA governing board. Most HOA's have strict rules about the size and placement of "auxiliary structures" such as storage sheds. If your neighbor's structure violates these rules, the shed might have to come down.

Q & A: My neighbor and I have a large tree that serves as part of the boundary line between our houses. If lightning strikes the tree and it falls on a parked car in the street in front of our homes, who is liable for the damage?

Both of you. In cases like this, shared ownership means shared responsibility. In reality, however, since many jurisdictions require car insurance, it is possible that the owner of the car would be compensated for the damages by his or her insurance company. Thus, in a situation like this, it is likely that neither of you will be out of pocket with respect to any damage to the car. Keep in mind, however, that owner of the damaged car would be in his or her rights if he or she decided to go after you, your neighbor, or both for damages.

Q & A: Would your answer change if the tree damaged a car in my driveway or may neighbor's?

Not really. Despite where the incident occurs, you and your neighbor will continue to share ownership rights in the property (the tree), as well as liability for any damages caused by the tree.

Q & A: My neighbor has a large tree in her backyard. What started as a small sapling when we first moved into the neighborhood has blossomed into a 30-foot maple tree? As you might imagine, some of the tree's branches are quite large and now hang well into my backyard, particularly my patio, where I have a small cooking area and some outdoor seating. My neighbor really likes this tree—and so do I—but we have been having a continuing dispute over whether I can trim limbs and leaves from the part of his tree that overlaps into my yard. What can I do?

Aside from a boundary tree, a tree is the property of the person upon whose land the trunk stands. That seems to be the situation you are describing with respect to your neighbor's tree.

The common law, however, as well as most local ordinances and statutes recognize your rights as landowner to cut off, sever, or otherwise eliminate, in any manner you deem expedient, any portion of overhanging branches of a tree standing on your neighbor's yard.

In most states, a property owner who learns of a neighbor's tree encroaching onto his property must first warn or give notice to the neighbor prior to starting to cutting the overhang, to give them a chance to fix the problem. There is no fixed rule how you warn or give notice to the neighbor, or how long you must wait for the neighbor to fix the problem before you act.

Q & A: **I am in the process of trimming the leaves and encroaching branches of my next-door neighbor's trees. Will there be a problem if the process forces me to go into my neighbor's yard to trim the trees?**

The general rule is that you can only trim the encroaching tree up to the boundary line. In addition, you must obtain permission before you enter the other owner's property. The one exception to this rule is that you don't have to obtain permission if the limbs pose a threat to cause "imminent and grave harm."

In addition, you can't cut down or neighbor's entire tree. Nor can you destroy the "structural integrity" or the "cosmetic symmetry" of the tree if you trim if improperly. If this is a worry, you might be best served by either consulting your local laws on this subject, or, better yet, hiring a professional tree trimming service to get the job done properly.

If you don't want to cut the branches and overhanging limbs yourself, or, you can't afford a professional tree trimming service, you might want consult with your local officials about what to do. For example, some jurisdictions employ an "Enforcement Officer" to perform the task of cutting down overhanging tree branches. For example, Section 312.4.4 of the Philadelphia, Pennsylvania Property Maintenance Code reads, in part,

"If a Property Owner fails to remove an Overhanging or Encroaching Tree within thirty (30) days after notice of a violation …. the Department is authorized to proceed to prune or remove the Overhanging or Encroaching Tree to the extent necessary to cure the violation..."

In addition to having the tree encroachment removed, in the appropriate case, the owner of the land encroached on may maintain an action for any damages your neighbor might have suffered. In some cases, the amount of damages may be hard to prove. In others, such as direct damage to your roof or gutters, you task may prove easier.

Q & A: I have just discovered that my neighbor's tree roots are damaging the foundation of my home? Can I make him take remedial action and cut down the roots?

In most states, you cannot force the landowner to cut down the tree roots. To protect your home, however, you do have the right to cut down some of the tree roots so long as you do not destroy or seriously damage your neighbor's tree. In cases like this, I suggest you consult with a professional tree cutting service.

Q & A: I have been living in my new home for about a year. I am about to have some exaction work done in my back yard and I just commissioned a survey. The results of the survey show that my neighbor's garage encroaches unto my back yard by about five feet. I don't think that's fair and I want my neighbor to tear down that part of the garage and remove it from my property. Naturally, my neighbor is reluctant to take on the expense. What should I do?

First, you should determine whether your property is subject to any earlier deed restrictions or other written agreements allowing the encroachment. A routine property search by an attorney can determine if such an agreement exists. If so, you may be out of luck. Keep in mind, however, if such an agreement does exist and it was not filed, or not filed properly, the law deems that you do not have "notice" of it. If you don't have notice, then the agreement does not apply to you.

At this point, if there is no agreement, or you have not been given notice of it, you basically have two choices:

- Sue your neighbor for damages.
- Sue for a mandatory injunction to compel your neighbor to tear down the portion of the structure.
- Do nothing.

The real question here is how important it is for you to force your neighbor to tear down a part of his or her garage? The answer might turn on much the encroachment affects your use and

83

enjoyment of your property. If, for example, your yard is a large one, then perhaps an encroachment of five feet is not that significant. On the other hand, if the lots in your area are smaller, then five feet could be a considerable amount of land. Based on your answer to this question, you might decide that a damages action is the best route to pursue.

Q & A: **I have a new house on a lot that has been professionally graded. Because of the excellent grading job, I have had few any problems with soil runoff. Last year, someone purchased the empty lot next door and had a house built. The problem is that my neighbor had his lot graded to a lower level than mine. Now much of the soil on the side of my house facing is constantly falling away. What should I do?**

The answer here may be a little unsettling. In situations like this the homeowner usually has two remedies: (1) suing for damages, or (2) getting an injunction to stop the action of your neighbor that is causing your loss of lateral support for your soil.

Some courts have held that where there is "an adequate remedy at law for damages", the plaintiff has no right to injunctive relief. As you might imagine for most homeowners, this hyper-technical rule makes little practical sense; suing and waiting to get damages is simply not going to suffice if your soil—and, perhaps—your house—is falling away in the process.

What should you do?

Here, your best bet is to seek immediate legal advice on what the courts in your area have decided in cases like this. In addition, you might want to contact your local homeowner's insurance agent to find out whether a situation like this is covered.

Q & A: I hired an independent contractor to perform some excavation around my home. After the work was completed, my neighbor has been complaining vocally about the soil dropping off from around his home. He is blaming the excavation work. I am afraid he may sue me. Shouldn't I be able to get off the hook since I did not do the work?

No. While even under common law rules, a landowner who negligently removes lateral support may be held liable for damages to the adjoining property, but under the "Independent Contactor Rule", a landowner who hires an independent contractor generally is not liable if the independent contractor negligently removes lateral support. The idea behind this rule was that the hiring party had no control over the manner in which the work was to be performed.

The "Independent Contractor Rule" has largely been supplanted by statute and now you, as an owner, can be held liable for any damages to your neighbor's property as a result of the excavation. Since your neighbor has not sued you yet, I suggest you contact the contractor so that the problem can be remedied now.

Q & A: Each year, my large family conducts a July 4th fireworks display at one of our homes. The financial responsibility for buying the fireworks is divided among family members. The fireworks are stored at the home of the

family member hosting the celebration. This year, it is my turn, and my spouse is concerned about any liability if there is an accident. My family likes to have fun, and we have never had an accident because we take the storage of our fireworks very seriously. Still, my spouse and her mother remain skeptical. Should I be concerned?

Yes. While is it fine that your family has a holiday tradition, fireworks, if handled improperly, can be very dangerous. As for your potential liability for money damages, even if you act with extreme caution and diligence. You might want to think about changing the family tradition and going as a family to a park where professionals are usually handling the fireworks. And get rid of any fireworks you have already stored.

Q & A: I live in a single home condominium community where most everyone gets along. I have a three-bedroom home with excellent views of a small lake. My new next door neighbor is thinking about adding an extra sunroom to his home that would effectively block my view of the lake. Since it's his property, I guess I am just out of luck.

Not necessarily. While the "Ancient Lights" doctrine has long died out, some communities have decided to revive the doctrine by adopting rules that may prohibit the obstruction of views. You might want to check your community's CC&R to find out of these rules apply to you. You might be able to save your view.

Trespassers

Trespass Law Generally pg. 88

Types of Civil Trespassers pg. 89

  People Who Take "Shortcuts" **pg.** 89

  People Who Use Your Property's Amenities   pg. 89

  People Who Encroach Upon Your Property pg. 90

Children and Trespassing pg. 90

Negligence pg. 92

Prerequisites to a Successful Trespass Action   pg. 92

Actions for Damages for Trespass   pg. 93

Types of Damages Awards Available pg. 94

Mistaken Trespass pg. 97

Persons Liable for Trespass pg. 98

Defenses to a Trespass Action pg. 98

Questions and Answers pg. 98

Trespass Law Generally

Simply stated, a trespasser is person who enters your property without your permission.

The word "trespass" is defined in different ways, some of them highly technical. For our purposes, trespass can be viewed as occurring when anyone crosses upon or through your land without your implied or express permission to do so.

In legal terminology, trespass on real estate is some physical invasion of, or unlawful entry on, the real property of another. For you to win a successful damage claim for trespass on your property, the damages don't have to be significant—damages are presumed in a trespass situation. Proving damages and getting a significant damage award, however, are not the same thing.

Not everyone who enters your property is a trespasser. You can have friends and guests come to see you ("invitees"), or persons who go to your property for particular purposes, such as mail carriers or delivery persons ("licensees").

Trespassers can be divided into two general categories. Most trespassers fit into the "civil" category; that is, they are not on your property to commit crimes or otherwise cause you harm—they simply are an annoyance.

"Criminal trespassers," the persons in the other general category—burglars, for example, make unauthorized entries onto your property for illegal reasons. Since criminal trespassers are covered by general criminal law rules, this guidebook will concentrate primarily on civil trespassers.

Types of Civil Trespassers

Most residential trespass situations involve one of three scenarios.

- People who take "shortcuts" across your property
- People who use your property's amenities without your permission
- People who encroach upon your property without your consent.

People Who Take Shortcuts

Some people cut through your property because the "shortcut" serves as a faster or more expedient route to some other destination—perhaps to a bus or light rail stop, a shopping area, a play area, or some other destination. This group of people may be your immediate neighbors, or others who either live in the neighborhood, or pass through it regularly.

These kinds of trespasses tend to be sporadic and generally last for short periods of time. Nevertheless, they can still be extremely aggravating

People Who Use Your Property's Amenities

People who use your property's amenities are usually a less significant category than people who take shortcuts across your property. They do things like routinely using your outdoor pool or deck, or a basketball or tennis court—without your permission, and most likely when you are not at home for extended periods of time. Taken to extremes, this kind of behavior can border on criminal.

Like those in the first category, these people usually represent a combination of your immediate neighbors, or people who somehow find out about the amenities from your neighbors, or their friends.

Because you are likely absent from your property when these kinds of activities occur, you probably only find out about them from other neighbors who observe or hear them, or because when you return home, you discover the trash or other debris these interlopers might have left.

People Who Encroach on Your Property

The third category of trespassers—usually your immediate neighbors—are people who encroach on some portions of your yard by storing their personal property, e.g., building materials, miscellaneous "junk", or automobiles. This can be the worst type of trespass because it is ongoing and it can deprive you of the use of your property for extended periods of time.

Children and Trespassing

With respect to trespass, children should be given greater care than adults in situations where as an owner or occupier of land you know or have reason to know of their presence on your property. The degree of care given to children should be in proportion to their ability to foresee and avoid the perils that may be encountered on your property.

For example, in many local communities, property owners who maintain outdoor pools, even with fenced-in yards, are required to place an additional fence around the pool area.

The pool fence requirement serves a two-fold purpose: keeping a barrier between your family and your lawful guests and the pool area; and serving as a kind of warning to others—including trespassers—that potential dangers exist if they come through the fence gate, or hop over the fence.

Of course, these fence "warnings" don't always work, especially when it comes to curious children. The traditional rules determining the duty and liability of a landowner to children used to depend upon the status of the child such as whether the child was an invitee, licensee, or common trespasser. Over time, these traditional rules were modified with the recognition of the principle of "attractive nuisance," e.g. an outdoor pool. According to the theory of attractive nuisance, a landowner was subject to liability for physical harm to children trespassing upon it, regardless of their status as trespassers, licensees, or invitees. Today, the only duty a landowner owes children who are trespassers is to not willfully or intentionally injure them.

Generally, the liability of a landowner with respect to a trespassing child depends upon: (1) the landowner's failure to take reasonable care against the foreseeable conduct of the trespassing child; and, (2) the need to balance the socially desirable policy of allowing a landowner to use the land in his/her own way against the humanitarian concern for the welfare of children. Most courts would find that a landowner who constructs and maintains a pool fence in accordance with established local rules would be seen as taking "reasonable care against the foreseeable conduct of a trespassing child." Only under the most extreme circumstances, would a landowner be expected to, for example, post a twenty-four guard at his home pool!

Where a child's conduct constitutes a serious violation of the law and the injury suffered by the child is the direct result of that violation, the court will not entertain a suit for injuries. Likewise, the primary responsibility of supervising and protecting children from injury rests with their parents or legal custodians. It is the duty of the parents to see that the child's behavior does not involve danger to the child and that they do not violate the law.

Negligence

Ordinary negligence rules determine the liability of a land owner for injuries to persons who occupy his or her land, even if they are trespassers. The simple definition of ordinary negligence is the failure to take the care that a reasonably cautious person usually takes. Legal scholars have developed several complex ways to describe negligence, some of them quite convoluted.

A simple way to describe the elements of negligence is to show (1) the existence of some duty; (2) a breach (violation of that duty); (3) a cause of action (injury resulting from breach of that duty); and (4) resultant damages.

Prerequisites to a Successful Trespass Action

There are certain essentials or prerequisites that you will need to meet if you want to pursue a successful trespass action. The primary one is that you must have actual or constructive possession of the property.

Generally speaking, under the concept of "constructive possession," the holder of the legal title to the property can sue a third party for trespass because his or her title to the property is superior to the wrong-doer.

In addition—you might be surprised to learn this—under some common law concepts, you don't have to "own" the property in the usual sense; to sue someone for trespass, you just have to have better rights than the second trespasser!

Lastly, and most importantly, in order to sue for trespass, someone must enter your land without your permission, and there must be some damage that results from that entrance. Trivial matters, such as someone tripping and falling on your grass, do not count as a trespass.

Actions for Damages for Trespass

While there is no universal rule for determining the amount of damages for trespass, the law presumes damages in every case. Accordingly, if you sue for trespass and you prevail, you will always be entitled to some damages, even though the amount of damages you will be awarded by the courts may be nominal.

There is no fixed rule for the measurement of damages in a trespass case. This means that the damages a court will award will vary according to the injury or harm caused due to the trespass.

When it measures damages, a court will examine the nature of the injury caused by the trespass, including whether the injury is permanent or temporary. The measure of damages for a temporary injury is the amount required for restoration or repair of the property. Both past and future damages may be recovered in permanent injury cases. Nominal damages may also be awarded in a temporary injury trespass

Types of Damage Awards Available

Of course, in the eyes of the law, just alleging damages in a trespass action is not enough; you still must provide sufficient evidence to show that you are entitled to damages.

If you are successful, the actual damages you *could* receive include:

- Diminution of the market value of your property.

- Costs of the restoration of any property damaged.

- Loss of the use of the property.

- Physical injury to any person or persons or to the land itself.

- Emotional distress without a physical injury to any person on the land.

- Discomfort and annoyance to you as property owner as a possessor of the property.

As you have probably noticed, some of these damage categories overlap.

Generally, it is the discretion of a court or a jury to decide the amount of damages. If the court's decision is appealed, a damage award will be set aside only if the appeal court finds the award unreasonable or disproportionate to the injury caused. Damages, even if they are nominal, are not always automatic.

For example, some courts will not award damages in a successful trespass in cases when they find that a trespass was not deliberate and where no damages or loss has happened. If you are thinking about pursuing a trespass action, you should take this view into account. Even in jurisdictions that award damages, in cases where no actual damage has occurred, nominal damages need not be awarded.

In case of a trespass that dispossesses you as an owner, damages would be an amount that would compensate you for the trespasser's use and occupation of your property, that is, the fair rental value. Usually, where an injury to a land resulting from a trespass is temporary and subject to restoration, the damages awarded would be the cost of restoring the property to its prior condition, but only where replacement or restoration costs are practical and reasonable.

Any loss of time for you as an owner of a personal property because of trespass will not be considered by the courts, except in extraordinary circumstances where you have unable to perform your work or a contract without the use of that property.

Different types of damages are granted in an action for trespass. They are actual damages, nominal damages, consequential damages, punitive or exemplary damages, and multiple damages.

Actual damages are compensatory damages for the actual damage that occurred. Nominal damages are awarded when a property owner cannot prove what actual damages occurred.

Consequential damages are damages awarded for all injuries resulting from a trespass. A person is responsible for all the consequences arising from his/her trespass onto another's property. A landowner may be entitled to punitive damages, in the case of intentional trespass, as the cost of restoration of the damage occurred to a property. As you might expect, the in this context, the "punitive damages" are awarded in cases of particularly outrageous trespasser conduct.

Multiple damages are awarded under certain circumstances in some jurisdictions by state statutes. Multiple damages are provided as deterrence from committing the offense in future.

Proof of damages need not be given in an exact or precise manner, but it is necessary to recover damages in an action for trespass. An award of damages for a trespass to real property must be supported by evidence of the value of property damaged or expenses incurred. What this means is that a trespasser cannot escape liability, even if there is uncertainty as to the extent of the value of damages.

The general principal is that the measure of damages in a trespass situation is the pecuniary loss resulting proximately from the injury. Here's an example:

Let's say you a single-family home and, for some reason, a third-party gains entry to that home without your knowledge or permission, and stays for a week and then leaves. It doesn't matter whether the third party acted maliciously, or even mistakenly. Those acts, entering illegally and staying would constitute trespass and would automatically trigger some liability for damages to **your** premises. But how much, and how would you calculate the amount?

In this case, a simple method of damage calculation would be to figure out how much it would cost to rent your premises on a daily, weekly, or monthly basis. Checking with a local real estate or rental agency would give you some idea regarding comparable rental costs for your property.

Let's say, further, that you find that in area comparable properties would rent for $1000 a month. Using that number, your trespasser would be liable to you for $250, plus the cost of any other damages he caused, i.e., breakage, vandalism, etc.

The real issue here, however, is not the calculation of damages, but first whether you can locate the third party for the purpose of serving him with legal process. Even if you do locate the person, and even if you win your case, it is likely under these circumstances that a person who "house-sits" illegally might not even have any collectable assets that you can seize to pay the damages.

Mistaken Trespass

You don't automatically get off the hook for a mistaken

trespass. In most jurisdictions today, a person will be liable for damages or a trespass, even if the trespass was committed by a mistake of law or a mistake of fact. Certain state statutes will allow a court to award nominal damages where the trespasser had probable cause, or an honest and reasonable belief that the land on which the trespass was committed was his/her own. Once again, you should check to discover if such a law exists in your area.

Persons Liable

Individual who commit an act of trespass, or causes a third party to do so, by intentionally entering unto your land is subject to liability for trespass.

Defenses to a Trespass Action

An alleged trespasser is not without legal defenses. Under some circumstances, the following defenses can be asserted by a person accused of trespass:

- Good faith.
- Superior title to the property.
- The person was acting under a court order.
- Statutory authorization.

Questions & Answers

Q &A: My neighbor has a number of large trees on his property. Sometimes when he cuts limbs from them, he leaves some of the lumber across my property line for storage. This situation has become increasingly annoying. What should I do?

It appears that your neighbor, for his own convenience, is encroaching on your land through a combination of piling logs onto it and using it for his truck. Under these circumstances, you are entitled to damages. In addition to asking him to refrain from entering on your property to store his logs, you should also ask him to refrain from using your property as his private storage area.

If your neighbor does not comply with your request, your first course of action is to complain to your local officials about your neighbor conducting a "nuisance" on your property. While what he is doing is technically a trespass, getting local officials involved might be enough to get the logs removed without you having to resort to the cost and expense of a legal action.

If your public officials balk at your request because they consider it a private matter not covered by local ordinances, your only recourse would be to pursue an action for trespass on your own, or hire an attorney to do it for you.

Q & A: **My neighbor loves the new drone technology. He already has purchased one equipped with a camera and he insists on flying it around the neighborhood where many of us—including me—have outdoor swimming pools. We have asked him to stop, but he insists on flying his drone. We don't know whether he is actually taking pictures of us and our yards, but we are getting fed up with what we all consider his bad manners and invasions of our privacy. Over the last few years I have read a couple of news articles about outraged neighbors actually shooting drones down and then destroying them. We don't want to go that far, but we are frustrated with our neighbor's behavior. What can we do?**

As drone technology continues to advance, some of its uses, especially with respect to hot-button issues like privacy, have been subject to controversy. For example, it is not yet clear whether drones are "aircraft", or something else.

Generally speaking, flying an aircraft over another's land is not a trespass unless the flight is conducted in such a manner or at such an altitude as to unreasonably interfere with the landowner's right of the use and enjoyment of his property. But these were developed over a time when drone technology did not exist.

So, the real question here, in modern times, is not whether your neighbor's done is considered "aircraft" under the old common law rules, but whether his operation of the drone interferes with your rights as a property owner.

For example, does your neighbor's drone fly so low that you and your family have the risk of being hit by it? If the drone is being used to take pictures of you and your family, does that interfere with your property rights? One would think so.

As a property owner, you have the right to have the peaceful enjoyment of your property, including a reasonable expectation of privacy. If your neighbor's drone is equipped with a camera and it is being used to take picture of you, your property and your family and friends, you might have a case for invasion of privacy.

In addition, if you are part of an HOA, you might join with your neighbors in trying to determine whether you can pursue this issue through the establishment of some additional "drone rules" in your CC&Rs. If you aren't part of an HOA, maybe it's time to put this matter before your public for discussion, and perhaps some legislation.

Q & A: I can't get my head around this "adverse possession" concept. What does all this this mean? If you are using property that is not yours, isn't that a trespass?

That is correct, but under our common law property rules, the second possessor (1st trespasser) still has a better right than the 2nd trespasser.

Here is an example: Let's assume you have taken over an adjacent "vacant lot" so you can cultivate a vegetable garden. The "true owner" is not around, and you have taken on unmistakable acts of exclusive custody of the area of property you use for your garden, including fencing it off. Unless the true owner comes back and takes steps to oust you, to the outside world, you are the true owner and have all the rights of a true owner, including the right to sue third parties who trespass on your property without your express permission. But if the true owner returns in an appropriate amount of time you—and your garden—can be ousted from the property.

NOTE: In a related peculiar twist, based on "adverse possession," if you stay on the property long enough and continue to control and occupy it for a sufficient period of time, you may be able to supplant the true owner's rights.

<u>Time of Possession</u>

In order to sue another for trespass against your property, you must be in possession of it—actual or constructive. If you need to regain possession of your property because the trespasser has taken it over, you will have sue in an action called "ejectment" to regain your property rights.

Title or Interest

Subject to the exceptions I noted above, proof of title to land (usually a deed), without proof of actual possession of the land is enough to bring a trespass action. Keep in mind, however, constructive possession of property without some kind of documentation, may be insufficient in the face of "adverse possession" or another adversarial situation.

Statute of Limitations

The time to bring a civil lawsuit, including an action for trespass, is not unlimited. These time limits, usually referred to as "statutes of limitation" vary from state to state, but are generally three to five years. In other words, once the "cause of action" accrues (meaning the initial act of trespass), statute of limitations governs the time limit in which you must file a lawsuit. If you don't, you lose your right to sue, at least for that particular trespass. The rules regarding statutes of limitations vary depending on whether the trespass is continuing or not continuing.

Where a trespass is continuing, each additional damage caused by it represents an additional cause of action, and until that continued trespass by adverse use ripens into a presumptive right and estate in the trespasser, the party injured may bring his trespass action.

Q & A I have just purchased a home with a working outdoor pool. The pool fence needs repair, but I travel a great deal and I have not yet made arrangements to have the fence repaired or replaced. There are a number of children in my neighborhood, but many of my neighbors already have pools. Should I be concerned?

Yes. If you pool already has a fence around it, even if the fence is in disrepair, it is likely because the local rules of your community require it. In addition, just because many of the neighborhood children have access to their pools, do be surprised if they prefer using yours, especially if you travel "a great deal" and they can be out of earshot of their parents if they use your pool. You should take steps to repair your fence immediately.

Chapter VII

Businesses in Residential Neighborhoods

Businesses in Your Neighborhood   pg. 105

Restrictions on the Use of the Business Owner's Home
pg. 106

Restrictions on Types of Business Activities pg. 106

Nuisances and Negligence   pg. 109

Questions and Answers pg. 110

Businesses in Your Neighborhood

A business operating near your single-family home or apartment can serve as both a blessing and a curse, often depending on what type of business is being conducted, the hours the business keeps, the noise the business creates or encourages, or the noxious odors the business emits.

Every business operation in a residential area must be viewed in context. If, for example, your neighbor is a writer, or someone operating an online business, or a portrait artist, the impact on you and your neighborhood likely will be insignificant.

On the other hand, if your neighbor is doing something else—like an auto-body shop, a small factory, a rock band, or something presumably illegal like running a gambling house, or promoting prostitution—then the impact on you and your neighbors would be highly objectionable. Businesses in residential neighborhoods can present additional annoyances, such as noise that occurs during garbage collection, high pedestrian and vehicular traffic, or unsightly and messy lawns and backyards.

For reasons like these, businesses usually are subject to a number of local laws and regulations. Home-based businesses—businesses located in residential areas—are subject to many of the law and regulations that apply to other business owners in non-residential areas.

Zoning laws affecting home-based business were once quite restrictive, but they have loosened up in recent years. Nevertheless, there are still some restrictions that home-based business owners and residential property owners should know about.

Restrictions on the Use of the Business Owner's Home

Local zoning restrictions regarding home-based businesses generally involve at least these categories:

- Limitations on signage
- Prohibition on types of commercial vehicles
- Restrictions on the number of business visitors
- Restrictions on the number of employees
- Restrictions on business parking
- Restrictions on noise, odor, etc.
- Restrictions on storage of certain materials

Restrictions on Types of Business Activities

Local home-based business zoning can be extensive and quite detailed. Below, for example, is a summary of the City of Tucson, Arizona's "home occupation" code:

- **A home occupation shall be clearly secondary to the residential use of the dwelling.**

- **A home occupation shall be conducted in such a manner that it is compatible with the residential character of the neighborhood in which it is located.**

- No more than twenty-five (25) percent of all buildings on the lot may be devoted to the home occupation. A detached accessory building of not more than two hundred (200) square feet in area may be used for such home occupation.

- Persons other than those residing in the dwelling shall not be employed in the home occupation, except that one (1) nonresident of the premises may be employed ... (portions omitted).

- Goods related to the home occupations shall not be visible from the street.

- Goods shall not be sold on the premises

- Outdoor storage of materials or equipment related to the home occupation activity is not permitted on the premises.

- Except for permitted signage, the home occupation use shall not substantially alter the exterior appearance or character of the residence in which it is conducted, either by exterior construction, lighting, graphics, or other means.

- No more than one (1) sign may be visible from the exterior of the property used as a home occupation. The sign shall not exceed one (1) square foot in size. Signs must also conform to Chapter 3 of the Tucson Code.

- A home occupation shall not create any nuisance, hazard, or other offensive condition, such as that resulting from noise, smoke, fumes, dust, odors, or other noxious emissions. Electrical or mechanical equipment that causes fluctuations in line voltage, creates any interference in either audio or video reception, or causes any perceivable vibration on adjacent properties is not permitted.

- No more than five (5) clients per day, and only one (1) client at a time, are allowed on site.

- Motor vehicle and bicycle parking is not required for home occupation. The home occupation may involve the use of no more than one (1) commercial vehicle for the transportation of goods or materials to and from the premises.

- The commercial vehicle is limited to a passenger car, van, or pickup truck. This vehicle may not be more than twenty (20) feet in overall length and not more than seven (7) feet in overall height and be parked be parked on private property in a carport or garage or shielded from view from adjoining properties by landscaping, fencing, or screening material. Motor vehicle and bicycle parking necessitated by the conduct of such home occupation shall be provided on site.

- **Automotive - Service and Repair, hair salon, and Medical Service uses are prohibited as home occupations.**

For another example of some local home-based zoning restrictions, **see Appendix I.**

Nuisances and Negligence

As with any other land use in a residential area, businesses also are subject to legal prohibitions against public and private nuisances. In addition, a business owner's careless behavior could be considered negligent and cause the business owner to be liable to you.

"Negligent" behavior is generally considered to be "the failure to take the care toward others which a reasonable or prudent person would do in like circumstances."

Assuming you can't get the business to stop or modify its operations, you as a homeowner are to:

- Consult with your local authorities to determine if the business operation is violation any zoning law or other regulation, such as the failure to secure the proper licenses.
- Consult with your local authorities to determine whether the business operation constitutes a "public nuisance," subjecting the owner to fines or injunctive relief.
- To the extent that the business operation is specifically affecting the use and enjoyment of your property, sue for

an injunction to stop, or modify the business owner's actions.
- Sue for damages, including the reduction in your property values (if you are a homeowner, not a tenant); lack of sleep; loss of the use of some or all your property; and legal expenses, if any.

If you win, some courts also will award damages for your mental anguish, sometimes referred to as "intentional infliction of mental distress."

Questions and Answers

Q & A: Who do I contact if there is a neighbor who is running a business out of his property? My neighbor seems to be using his property to detail cars all day. It's totally obnoxious and produces noise pollution and air pollution to our little neighborhood. Is this legal?

If a one-on-one conversation with your neighbor won't work, based on where you live, you should consider contacting your county or city zoning office. It is highly likely that your local code will contain prohibitions against the types of businesses that can be conducted in a residential area; noises from those businesses; as well as the times those businesses can be run.

Q & A: My neighbor is a lawyer who runs his practice out of his home? Is this legal?

All home-based businesses are not prohibited. In this case,

unless your neighbor's business activities promote excessive noise or vehicular traffic, or involves prohibited signage, it is likely that your neighbor's law practice is allowed.

Q & A: I want to run a business out of my home. Are there any permits or licenses I need to get before I open?

It depends on the business. As with my response to the lawyer question above, if your business does not create excessive noise, or vehicular traffic, or uses prohibited signage, or is absolutely prohibited (for example, a car repair business), you probably don't require any additional permits or licenses other than the usual professional licenses you will need to conduct your business.

Q & A: I live across the street from a home-based business which seems to be generating a lot of automobile traffic at odd hours. I am concerned about two things: (1) the noise and disruption generated by the automobile traffic; and (2) whether the "business" is some illegal operation like drug sales, etc. What should I do?

You can find the answers to the first part of your question by taking a look at your local zoning laws, or CC&Rs.

As for the second part of your question, you might think about conferring with your local police department. You should be careful here, however. If your accusation regarding your neighbor's alleged illegal is unreasonable or unfounded, you might be facing a lawsuit for slander.

Q & A: Home-based businesses are allowed in our neighborhood. One of my neighbors has erected a rather large neon sign that blinks regularly and disturbs my sleep. What should I do?

Based on your description of the sign, it probably is prohibited under local zoning law or CC&R. Even if neither of these sources are available to you (I doubt it), you still probably can make a case that your neighbor is creating a nuisance.

Q & A: I am from the Midwest and have recently located to the Southwest. I live in a residential area that allows property owners to keep and raise a limited amount of chickens. Lately, however, it seems that my neighbor is starting a small chicken "farm." What should I do?

Many jurisdictions allow the property owner to do what you have just described, often allowing a real property tax deduction in such cases. You need to consult the local rules regarding what a "limited amount" of chickens is. If your neighbor meets the appropriate criteria, your remedies may be limited. Keep in mind, however, that even a "legal" operation, if operated negligently, can become the basis for a nuisance action.

Glossary of Selected Legal Terms

Adjoining Landowners

The owners of lands that are separated by a common boundary.

Alternative Dispute Resolution (ADR)

The procedure for settling disputes without litigation, such as arbitration, mediation, or negotiation.

CC&Rs

Real property deed covenants or declarations covering land use conditions, covenants, and restrictions, used often in connection to Home Owners' Associations (HOAs).

Common Law

The part of English Law developed over time from the rulings of judges, as opposed to law embodied in statutes passed by legislatures, or law embodied in a written constitution.

Complaint

Used in law suit and the first formal legal document that sets out the facts and legal reasons that the filing party (the "Plaintiff") believes are sufficient to support a claim against whom the claim is brought (the "Defendant").

Homeowners Association (HOA)

An organization in a subdivision, planned community or condominium that makes and enforces rules for the property in its jurisdiction.

Injunction

A judicial order or procedure requiring a person or persons to whom it is directed to do a particular act or to refrain from doing a particular act.

Negligence

Generally, the failure to take the care toward others which a reasonable or prudent person would do in like circumstances.

Nuisance

An obnoxious person, thing, or activity that reduces another person's ability to enjoy the peaceful enjoyment of his real or personal property.

Punitive Damages

Monetary compensation awarded to an injured party that goes beyond that which is necessary to compensate the individual for losses and that is intended to punish the wrongdoer.

Service Animal

Any guide dog, signal dog, or any other animal trained to do work or perform tasks for the benefit of an individual with a disability.

Trespass

To enter a person's land or property without their permission. Trespass can be characterized as civil in nature (usually involving a fine or injunction), or criminal in nature (possibly involving fines and imprisonment).

Zoning

The separation and division of a municipality into districts, the regulation of buildings and structures in such districts in accordance with their construction and the nature and extent of their use, and the dedication of such districts to particular uses designed to serve the general welfare.

Additional Resources

In addition to the information I have provided, the following publications and websites might be helpful to you when you try to deal with neighbor disputes:

American Bar Association, Chapter 7, "Love Thy Neighbor: "How to Keep Petty Annoyances from Turning in to Major Headaches"

www.americanbar.org/content/dam/aba/migrated/.../chapter 7.pdf

HOA-USA, www.hoa-usa.com

NOLO Press, headquartered in California, provides many useful publications, including, Dog Law and Neighbor Law.

FindLaw, www.findlaw.org

USLegal, www.uslegal.org

Homeownersassociationdirectory.com

"Effective Deer Fences," Dr. Leonard Perry, Extension Professor University of Vermont. http://pss.uvm.edu/ppp/articles/deerfences.html.

Appendices

Appendix A:
List of links to state-by-state HOA laws

Appendix B:
"Top 7 Insane Homeowners Association Rules"

Appendix C:
Selected Deed Restrictions and Covenants

Appendix D:
Smalls Claims Courts Statutory Limits

Appendix E:
Dog Bite Costs

Appendix F:
Partition Fence Agreement

Appendix G:
Adverse Possession Statutes of Limitation

Appendix H:
Easement Agreement for Light, Air & View

Appendix I:
Local Home-based Business Zoning

Appendix A

Links to State HOA Laws

Below you will find links to state homeowner and condominium association laws. Some websites, including, for example, HOA Member Services (HOAmember.site-ym.com) provide condensed versions of state HOA laws for a fee.

Alabama
http://www.legislature.state.al.us/CodeofAlabama/1975/135208.htm

Alaska
http://www.touchngo.com/lglcntr/akstats/Statutes/Title34/Chapter08.htm
http://www.maxwellandmorgan.com/resources/arizona_nonprofit_corporation_act

Arizona
http://www.azleg.gov/FormatDocument.asp?inDoc=/ars/33/01201.htm&Title=33&DocType=ARS
http://www.maxwellandmorgan.com/resources/arizona_nonprofit_corporation_act

Arkansas
http://www.arkleg.state.ar.us/SearchCenter/Pages/ArkansasCodeSearchResultPage.aspx

California
http://www.leginfo.ca.gov/calaw.html
http://www.epsten.com/files/dsa/3/2011Davis-StirlingBookforEGHWebsite.4df004b525a4e.pdf

Colorado
http://www.lexisnexis.com/hottopics/Colorado/
http://www.cohoalaw.com/CCIOA%20-%202006%20annotated.pdf

Connecticut
http://www.cga.ct.gov/current/pub/titles.htm
http://www.cga.ct.gov/current/pub/title47.htm

Delaware
http://delcode.delaware.gov/
http://delcode.delaware.gov/title25/index.shtml

Washington, D.C.
http://www.schildlaw.com/dccondolaw-tab.htm

Florida
http://www.flsenate.gov/Laws/Statutes/?from500=yes#TitleXLhttp://archive.flsenate.gov/statutes/index.cfm?m&App_mode=Display_Statute&URL=Ch0718/titl0718.htm&StatuteYear=2005&Title=-%3E2005-%3EChapter%20718

Georgia
http://www.cai-georgia.org/pdfs/Georgia_Condominium_Act.pdforgia

Hawaii
http://www.capitol.hawaii.gov/

http://www.capitol.hawaii.gov/hrscurrent/Vol12_Ch0501-0588/HRS0514A/HRS_0514A-.htm

Idaho
http://www.legislature.idaho.gov/idstat/TOC/IDStatutesTOC.htm
http://www.legislature.idaho.gov/idstat/Title55/T55CH15.htm

Illinois
http://www.ilga.gov/legislation/ilcs/ilcs2.asp?ChapterID=62

Indiana
http://www.in.gov/legislative/ic/code/title32/ar25/

Iowa
http://search.legis.state.ia.us/NXT/gateway.dll?f=templates&fn=default.htm

Kansas
http://www.kslegislature.org/li/b2011_12/statute/

Kentucky
http://www.lrc.state.ky.us/krs/titles.htm

Louisiana
http://www.legis.state.la.us/lss/lss.asp?doc=106629

Maine
http://www.mainelegislature.org/legis/statutes/33/title33ch0sec0.html

Maryland
http://mlis.state.md.us/2008rs/statutes/grp_idx.htm
http://www.sos.state.md.us/registrations/condominiumbooklet.pdf

Massachusetts
http://www.malegislature.gov/Laws/GeneralLaws
http://www.malegislature.gov/Laws/GeneralLaws/PartII/TitleI/Chapter183a

Michigan
http://www.legislature.mi.gov/(S(atur4mr2edtsqu55byebxn45))/mileg.aspx?page=chapterindex
http://www.legislature.mi.gov/(S(bae1d055nsbb4pmtxbdvyt55))/mileg.aspx?page=getObject&objectName=mcl-Act-59-of-1978

Minnesota
https://www.revisor.mn.gov/statutes/?view=part&start=500&close=515b
https://www.revisor.mn.gov/statutes/?id=515a

Mississippi
http://www.mscode.com/free/statutes/89/009/index.htm

Missouri
http://www.moga.mo.gov/STATUTES/STATUTES.HTM#T29

Montana
http://data.opi.mt.gov/bills/mca_toc/70.htm
http://data.opi.mt.gov/bills/mca_toc/70_23.htm

Nebraska
http://nebraskalegislature.gov/laws/browse-chapters.php?chapter=69
http://uniweb.legislature.ne.gov/laws/search_range_statute.php?begin_section=76-801&end_section=76-894

Nevada
http://www.leg.state.nv.us/NRS/Index.cfm
http://www.leg.state.nv.us/nrs/nrs-117.html
http://www.leg.state.nv.us/NRS/NRS-116.html

New Hampshire
http://www.gencourt.state.nh.us/rsa/html/nhtoc.htm
http://www.gencourt.state.nh.us/rsa/html/xxxi/356-b/356-b-mrg.htm

New Jersey
http://lis.njleg.state.nj.us/cgi-bin/om_isapi.dll?clientID=510748&depth=2&expandheadings=off&headingswithhits=on&infobase=statutes.nfo&softpage=TOC_Frame_Pg42

New Mexico
http://www.nmonesource.com/nmpublic/gateway.dll/?f=templates&fn=default.htm

New York
http://public.leginfo.state.ny.us/menugetf.cgi?COMMONQUERY=LAWS

North Carolina
http://www.ncga.state.nc.us/gascripts/statutes/statutestoc.pl
http://www.ncleg.net/gascripts/Statutes/StatutesTOC.pl?Chapter=0047C
    http://www.ncleg.net/gascripts/Statutes/StatutesTOC.pl?Chapter=0047A

North Dakota
http://www.legis.nd.gov/cencode/t47.html
http://www.legis.nd.gov/cencode/t47c04-1.pdf

Ohio
http://codes.ohio.gov/orc/53
http://codes.ohio.gov/orc/5311

Oklahoma
http://www.oklegislature.gov/osStatuesTitle.html

Oregon
http://landru.leg.state.or.us/ors/
http://www.leg.state.or.us/ors/100.html

Pennsylvania
http://www.legis.state.pa.us/WU01/LI/LI/CT/HTM/68/68.HTM
http://www.pacondolaw.com/statutes_uca1.html

Rhode Island
http://webserver.rilin.state.ri.us/Statutes/TITLE34/INDEX.HTM
http://webserver.rilin.state.ri.us/Statutes/TITLE34/34-36/INDEX.HTM

South Carolina
http://www.scstatehouse.gov/code/statmast.php

South Dakota
http://legis.state.sd.us/statutes/DisplayStatute.aspx?Type=Statute&Statute=43
http://legis.state.sd.us/statutes/DisplayStatute.aspx?Type=Statute&Statute=43-15A

Tennessee
http://www.lexisnexis.com/hottopics/tncode/

Texas

http://www.statutes.legis.state.tx.us/?link=PR
http://www.statutes.legis.state.tx.us/Docs/PR/pdf/PR.82.pdf
http://www.statutes.legis.state.tx.us/Docs/PR/pdf/PR.209.pdf

Utah

http://www.le.state.ut.us/code/code.htm

Vermont

http://www.leg.state.vt.us/statutes/chapters.cfm?Title=27
http://www.leg.state.vt.us/statutes/sections.cfm?Title=27&Chapter=015
http://www.leg.state.vt.us/statutes/chapters.cfm?Title=27A

Virginia

http://leg1.state.va.us/cgi-bin/legp504.exe?000+cod+TOC5500000
http://leg1.state.va.us/cgi-bin/legp504.exe?000+cod+TOC55000000004000020000000
http://leg1.state.va.us/cgi-bin/legp504.exe?000+cod+TOC55000000004000010000000

Washington

http://apps.leg.wa.gov/rcw/
http://apps.leg.wa.gov/rcw/default.aspx?cite=64.34

West Virginia

http://www.legis.state.wv.us/WVCODE/code.cfm?chap=36b&art=1
http://www.legis.state.wv.us/WVCODE/code.cfm?chap=36a&art=1

Wisconsin

http://docs.legis.wisconsin.gov/statutes/prefaces/toc

Appendix B

"Top 7 Insane Homeowners Association Rules"

CC&Rs can be very restrictive, and it is important to know all the rules, because failure to do so can cost you time and money. For example, witness this humorous take on "tricky" CC&Rs in an in article published in *TheWeek.com* (December 9, 2009)

The astonishingly restrictive ways of homeowners' associations (HOAs) came under scrutiny this month when a Sussex Square, Virginia HOA demanded that a 90-year-old World War II vet remove an unapproved flag pole from his front yard. After receiving support from members of Congress, and even the Obama administration, Medal of Honor recipient Van T. Barfoot, who once singlehandedly took on three Nazi tanks, triumphed in his quest to fly Old Glory. Other homeowners haven't been as lucky in their battles against their own HOAs' "fascist" rules. Here are seven of the most controversial commandments:

1. Thou shalt not plant too many roses. A Rancho Santa Fe, California, homeowners' association targeted Jeffery DeMarco for exceeding the prescribed number of rose bushes allowed on his four-acre property. When DeMarco balked, the HOA levied monthly fines, threatened foreclosure, and ultimately defeated DeMarco in court. After a judge ruled that the willful rose enthusiast had violated the community's architecture design rules, DeMarco was forced to pay the HOA's $70,000 legal bill — and lost his home to the bank.

2. **Thou shalt not use "inconsistent" shingles — even after a plane destroys thy house**

After a plane crashed into the Sanford, Florida, home of Joe Woodard, killing his wife, Janise, and their infant son, he decided to rebuild a new home on the same lot. But his reconstruction came to a screeching halt when his HOA informed him that he'd positioned the new structure unacceptably and failed to achieve a perfect shingle match with his neighbors' homes. Threatened with a lawsuit, the grieving widower told a local reporter that he'd hoped to change things up to avoid "reliving" painful memories—but eventually capitulated to the unsympathetic HOA.

3. **Thou shalt not post a "For Sale" sign**

When Denise Hicks placed a "For Sale" sign in front of her Lebanon, Tennessee, residence, the Spence Creek homeowners association quickly reprimanded her for a breach of contract, citing a rule prohibiting signs, banners or billboards. Ultimately, Hicks was forced to display her realtor's signs in her home's windows, hidden from view.

4. **Thou shalt not offer thy homeless granddaughter shelter**

Assuming guardianship of their six-year-old granddaughter, Kimberly, after her drug-addict mother was ruled unfit, Jimmy and Judy Stuttler brought the child to live with them in their Clearwater, Florida, retirement village. Since Kimberly was not technically "over 55" or arguably "retired," the alarmed HOA tried to force the girl out. Attempting to move, the Stuttlers failed to sell their home even after slashing its price from $250,000 to

$129,000 and were eventually sued by the HOA. Kimberley's fate is now in the hands of the courts.

5. **Thou must carry thy dog at all times**
Pamela McMahan, a geriatric who walks with a cane, was fined $25 every time she failed to carry her cocker spaniel through the lobby of her Long Beach, California condominium, which stipulates that pets' feet must never touch the floor of common areas. "There are too many things going on in the lobby," said Stormy Jech, the building's assistant property manager. "The dog might jump on someone or go to the bathroom." After racking up hundreds of dollars in fines, McMahan was forced to move.

6. **No smoking—even in thine own bathroom**
HOAs' ban on smoking in all public areas—including balconies, patios, courtyards, and swimming pool area—has recently been extended into residents' homes. Citing the negative health effects of secondhand smoke, multiple court hearings have ruled in favor of HOAs. As Realty Times points out, "The Constitution does not guarantee Americans the right to smoke in their homes...."

7. **Thou shalt maintain a consistently green lawn**
The Beacon Woods Civic Association in Bayonet Point, Florida, took 66-year old resident Joseph Prudente to court for failing to properly maintain his lawn after a $600-per-month increase to his adjustable rate mortgage threw him on hard times.

Though Prudente was ultimately jailed for failing to resod his lawn, other members of the community took pity on the faulty landscaper, and paid for new sod, flowers, mulching, and functioning sprinklers. Their charity was enough to spring their elderly neighbor from the slammer, but Prudente still faces court and association fines.

Appendix C

Selected Deed Covenants & Restrictions

Source: www.wsmaonline.org

Williamsburg Settlement

Homeowners Association

Katy, Texas

Declaration of Restrictions

Article 13. Fences and Walls

"No fence, wall, hedge, gas meter or other structure or mass planting shall be placed or be permitted to remain on any lot at a location between any boundary of such lot which is adjacent to any street or streets and the building set-back line affecting such lot...., unless such structure or mass planting and its location shall be approved by the hereinafter named Association. All fences and walls located on any lot...shall be six (6) feet in height above ground level, unless otherwise approved by the Association."

Article 15. Outside Clothes Drying

"The drying of clothes in general view is prohibited, and the owners or occupants of any lot desiring to dry clothes outside shall construct and maintain suitable screening enclosures for such use, which enclosures must be approved by the hereinafter named Association."

Appendix D

Smalls Claims Courts Statutory Limits

Most small claims courts periodically raise their small claims limits and amend their procedures. If you plan to sue in a small claims court, don't forget to the up to date information on latest claim limits and court procedures.

State	Amount	State	Amount
Alabama	$3000	Montana	$3000
Alaska	$10,000	Nebraska	$3500
Arizona	$2500	Nevada	$5000
California	$7500*	New Hampshire	$7500
Colorado	$7500	New Jersey	$3000*
Connecticut	$5000*	New Mexico	$10,000
Delaware	$15,000	New York	$5000
D.C.	$5000	North Carolina	$5000
Florida	$5000	Ohio	$3000
Georgia	$15,000*	Oklahoma	$6000
Hawaii	$3500*	Oregon	$7500
Idaho	$5000	Pennsylvania	$8000
Illinois	$10,000	Rhode Island	$2500
Indiana	$6000	South Carolina	$7500
Iowa	$5000	South Dakota	$12,000
Kansas	$4000	Tennessee	$25,000*
Kentucky	$1500	Texas	$10,000
Louisiana	$3000*	Utah	$10,000
Maine	$6000	Vermont	$5000
Maryland	$5000	Virginia	$5000
Massachusetts	$7000*	Washington	$5000
Michigan	$3000	West Virginia	$5000
Minnesota	$7500*	Wisconsin	$5000
Mississippi	$3500	Wyoming	$5000*
Missouri	$3000		

*Some state small claims courts rules contain differences regarding limitations on limitations on types of claims filed; limits regarding what local entities can file and for how much, no limits in landlord-tenant cases, or property damage caused by a motor vehicle, etc.

Appendix E
Dog Bite Costs[1]

Although state laws vary, pet owners are usually considered legally responsible for their dog's behavior, and in most bite cases, are required to pay all medical bills as well as lost wages resulting from the attack. They can also be ordered to pay for the bite-victim's pain and suffering. If the dog owner is particularly negligent—such as letting a dog known to be dangerous run loose—there might be multiple or punitive damages, as well as separate criminal charges.

Typical Costs: A simple dog bite case, with basic medical care and some time off work but no major injury, permanent damage or scarring, could be handled in <u>Small Claims Court, typica</u>lly without lawyers. Filing fees and other costs for the claimant can run **$20-$320** or more, but can be repaid by the defendant if you win. Nolo Press describes a hypothetical dog bite case.

For a dog bite incident with serious injury, mental aggravation and hospital bills, most lawyers work on a contingency basis; they don't get paid until you do, and then they take anywhere from 30-40 percent of the money received. (Generally, the lawyer's percentage is lower if the case is settled pretrial, and higher if it goes to trial or is appealed.) If you don't get any money in a settlement or court judgment, you don't owe any legal fees. Some lawyers charge a percentage of all money received; others take their percentage after the medical bills are paid. In a case with **$50,000 i**n medical costs and a **$100,000** settlement, a lawyer charging 33 percent of the total gets **$33,000.**

There are also court costs, expert witness fees, investigation charges, clerical labor, and other expenses. In most states your attorney will pay these and be reimbursed out of the final settlement/judgment. These costs start around **$1,000-$2,000** for an extremely simple case but can go much higher, depending on what's involved. In some states, your lawyer can advance you the money for your medical bills and be reimbursed out of the settlement/judgment. If medical costs are paid by your health insurance, that company will be reimbursed out of the settlement/judgment.

A lawyer may charge based on an hourly rate of **$100-$300** or more, billed monthly and charged whether or not your case is successful. This could run **$5,000-$25,000** and up; however, if you can't find a personal injury lawyer to take your lawsuit on a contingency fee basis, it's usually a sign that you don't have a good case.

- For a dog owner with homeowner's/liability insurance, usually the insurance company will provide defense attorneys, and will negotiate and pay a settlement in a dog bite lawsuit (unless the policy has a clause specifically excluding dog bites). These legal defense costs can easily run **$10,000-$50,000** or more and have gone as high as **$100,000-$200,000** and up. Dog owners without insurance must pay legal fees and expenses plus any amounts awarded to the defendant, and could lose their personal assets if the court rules against them. Settlements or judgements awarded in dog bite cases can be anywhere from **$5,000-$500,000** or more depending on circumstances.

[1]**Source:** www.personalfinance@Costhelper.com

Appendix F

Partition Fence Agreements

NOTE: Property owners usually do not enter into partition fence agreements on a regular basis. The form below should serve as both a template if you are thinking about entering into one, or model of what an existing partition fenced agreement might look like.

Partition Fence Agreement

This Partition Fence Agreement ("Agreement") is dated _____, 20__, by and between ___[Name, address]___ ("First Party") and ___[Name, address]___ (Second Party)

1. First Party is the owner of the property

    described as ___[address]___ ("First Party's Property").

2. Second Party is the owner of the property described as ___[address]___ ("Second Party's Property").

3. First Party and Second Party want to erect a fence between their respective properties.

4. In consideration of the mutual covenants and conditions hereinafter set forth in this Agreement, and for other good and valuable consideration, the receipt of which is hereby acknowledged, the parties agree as follows:

5. The parties agree to erect a fence ("Fence") along the boundary line between the First Party's Property and the Second Party's Property. The Parties will use their best efforts to ensure that construction of the Fence commences on or before _____ and is completed no later than _____.

6. The Parties agree to share the costs of the Fence equally, and they acknowledge and agree that the cost of the Fence shall be no more than $_____.

7. The Fence shall be constructed using **[describe type of materials to be used]** Materials and shall be constructed according to the plans and specifications attached hereto as Exhibit A.
8. The Parties agree to share equally the cost of the Fence, maintenance, upkeep, and repairs of the Fence from time to time. To avoid any conflict on the issue, the Parties agree to pay their 50% share of Fence construction to the agreed upon contractor in advance the work being done to ensure that there are no leftover costs associated with the initial construction period.
9. This Agreement shall inure to the benefit of and be binding upon the respective heir, executors, administrators and assigns of each of the parties hereto.
10. This Agreement sets forth the entire agreement between the Parties, and replaces and supersedes any previous agreement between the Parties, whether oral or written. The Parties further agree that no amendment to this Agreement shall be binding upon the parties unless it is in writing and executed by both Parties. Any dispute under this Agreement must be brought within the state of _____.

    IN WITNESS, WHEREOF, this Agreement has been executed by the Parties as of the date above.

_____   _____
First Party   **Second Party**

_____   _____
Witness   **Witness**

<u>Exhibit A</u> **[Agreement plans and specifications]**

NOTE: If you want future parties (i.e., persons who buy either property in the future), it is probably best to record a Partition Fence Agreement with the appropriate local recording office, usually the County Recorder.

Appendix G

Adverse Possession Statutes of Limitations

NOTE: Adverse possession statutes vary greatly from state to state and are subject to amendment. Sometimes the time required to secure possession is based on whether the occupier has as deed –even if a defective deed ("color of title"), or has paid taxes. Accordingly, if you intend file a claim for adverse possession, or defend one, you should check your current state law. Accordingly, this listing is not intended to be comprehensive.

State	Years Required
Alabama	10
Alaska	10; 7
Arizona	10; 7
Arkansas	7
California	5
Colorado	18; 7
Connecticut	15
Delaware	20
District of Columbia	15
Florida	7
Georgia	7
Hawaii	20
Idaho	20
Illinois	20; 7
Indiana	10
Iowa	10
Kansas	15
Kentucky	15; 7
Louisiana	30; 10
Maine	20
Maryland	20
Massachusetts	20

Michigan	15
Mississippi	10
Missouri	10
Montana	5
Nebraska	10
Nevada	15; 5
New Hampshire	20
New Jersey	30
New Mexico	10
New York	10
North Carolina	20; 7
North Dakota	20: 10
Ohio	21
Oklahoma	15
Oregon	10
Pennsylvania	21
Rhode Island	10
South Carolina	10
South Dakota	15; 15
Tennessee	7
Texas	10; 5
Utah	7
Vermont	15
Virginia	15
Washington	10; 7
West Virginia	10
Wisconsin	20; 10; 7
Wyoming	10

Appendix H

Easement Agreement for Light, Air & View

Grantor reserves however to (himself or herself), as and for an appurtenance to the real property described as follows: _____, and for any part of it to receive light, air, and an unobstructed view over that part of the above-described real property, to the extent that such light, air, and view will be received and enjoyed by limiting any structure, fence, trees, or shrubs on the property, or any part of it, to a height not extending above a horizontal plane _____ feet above the level of the sidewalk of _____ (street), as the sidewalk level now exists at the junction of the _____ (northern/southern/eastern/western) and _____ (northern/southern/eastern/western) boundary lines of the above-described property. Any obstruction of such view above such horizontal plane, except _____ (specify existing obstructions and other desired exceptions, including any exceptions to be allowed for radio and television receiving devices, power and telephone poles and lines other than those required to be buried, and required flues or vents, as well as fixtures required under any building regulations), shall be considered an unauthorized interference with such right or easement and shall be removed on demand at the expense of grantee, and (his or her) heirs, successors, and assigns in the ownership of the above-described real property or any part of it.

_____   Date: _____
Signature

_____
_____
Witnesses Signatures   Date: _____

NOTE: If you want future parties (i.e., persons who buy either property in the future), it is probably best to record an Easement Agreement for Light, Air & View with the appropriate local recording office, usually the County Recorder.

Appendix I

Local Home-based Business Zoning

Local home-based business zoning can be extensive and quite detailed. Below, for example, is an occupation code:

1. Home occupation shall be clearly secondary to the residential use of the dwelling.
2. A home occupation shall be conducted in such a manner that it is compatible with the residential character of the neighborhood in which it is located.
3. No more than twenty-five (25) percent of all buildings on the lot may be devoted to the home occupation. A detached accessory building of not more than two hundred (200) square feet in area may be used for such home occupation.
4. Persons other than those residing in the dwelling shall not be employed in the home occupation, except that one (1) nonresident of the premises may be employed ... Goods related to the home occupation shall not be visible from the street.
5. Goods shall not be sold on the premises.
6. Outdoor storage of materials or equipment related to the home occupation activity is not permitted on the premises.
7. Except for permitted signage, the home occupation use shall not substantially alter the exterior appearance or character of the residence in which it is conducted, either by exterior construction, lighting, graphics, or other means.
8. No more than one (1) sign may be visible from the exterior of the property used as a home occupation. The sign shall not exceed one (1) square foot in size. Signs must also conform to Chapter 3 of the Tucson Code.
9. A home occupation shall not create any nuisance, hazard, or other offensive condition, such as that

10. resulting from noise, smoke, fumes, dust, odors, or other noxious emissions. Electrical or mechanical equipment that causes

    fluctuations in line voltage, creates any interference in either audio or video reception, or causes any perceivable vibration on adjacent properties is not permitted.

11. No more than five (5) clients per day, and only one (1) client at a time, are allowed on site.

12. Motor vehicle and bicycle parking is not required for home occupation - general application. The home occupation may involve the use of no more than one (1) commercial vehicle for the transportation of goods or materials to and from the premises. The commercial vehicle is limited to a passenger car, van, or pickup truck. This vehicle may not be more than twenty (20) feet in overall length and not more than seven (7) feet in overall height and must be parked on private property in a carport or garage or shielded from view from adjoining properties by landscaping, fencing, or screening material. Motor vehicle and bicycle parking necessitated by the conduct of such home occupation shall be provided on site.

13. Automotive - Service and Repair, hair salon, and Medical Service uses are prohibited as home occupations.

ABOUT THE AUTHOR

FREDERIC WHITE has practiced and written in the area of property, particularly landlord tenant relations, zoning, and land use control for over forty years. In addition, he has served on the faculties of three American Bar Association accredited law schools in three separate states, two of them as Dean. He is a graduate of the Columbia University School of Law and is the holder of the *"Distinguished Columbian in Teaching Award."*

In addition to his law practice and law teaching duties, he also has served as a grand jury foreman, a bar review course lecturer, a Continuing Legal Education lecturer, a Public Member of the United States Department of State Foreign Service Selection Board, and as a member of the American Bar Association Law School Accreditation Committee. He is also the author of <u>Ohio Landlord Tenant Law</u> (Thomson Reuters), a book tailored for use by lawyers and judges, as well as laypersons.

Other Books by Frederic White

Property Related

OHIO LANDLORD TENANT LAW

Ohio Landlord Tenant Law examines all aspects of the Landlord-Tenant Relationship. Its easy to-read question and answer format presents situations that landlords and tenants are likely to encounter. The book also includes selected Ohio Revised Code provisions that are similar to such provisions in other states. Topics include: • Lease applications • Lease Agreements • Forms for Pleadings and Tenant and Landlord Letters • Fair Housing Rent Deposits • Insurance & Taxes • Rent & Security Evictions • Tenant & Landlord Liability

Other Books by Frederic White

Fiction and Humor

LAW SCHOOL FOLLIES

Lawyers hold a particular place in American culture. We hate to love them. We love to hate them. This book pokes fun at the sometimes-bizarre circumstances that surround lawyers and legal education, including prickly law faculty; eccentric and absent-minded profs; nervous and unpredictable students; overbearing "helicopter" parents; conniving administrators; false alarms and surprise appearances.

Tenure Blues: A Soap Opera

Sex, money, bad faith, laughter, power struggles betrayal, politics—even death—at a law school. Who knew? Three bright young professors all vie for promotion and tenure at a law school. Not unusual, except in this case all three of them have secrets that could threaten their careers as well as their personal lives. Only one person—the law dean's son—knows all their secrets. Suddenly, he winds up dead. Who's to blame?

Law School Follies and **Tenure Blues** are available at **Amazon.com** in both print and Kindle versions!

www.ingramcontent.com/pod-product-compliance
Lightning Source LLC
Chambersburg PA
CBHW070248190526
45169CB00001B/338